DANIEL PLOOF

ATTRIBUTES OF A *Godly Man*

40-DAYS IN THE WILDERNESS
DEVOTIONAL SERIES

GALLATIN, TENNESSEE

Attributes of a Godly Man
Copyright © 2023 by Daniel Ploof

Psalm51 PUBLISHING

All Rights Reserved. No part of this publication may be reproduced, distributed, or transmitted in any form or by any means, including photocopying, recording, or other electronic or mechanical methods, without the prior written permission of the publisher, except as permitted by U.S. copyright law.

Library of Congress Control Number: 2023921190

ISBN: 978-1-7373673-4-5 (print)
ISBN: 978-1-7373673-5-2 (e-book)
ISBN: 978-1-7373673-6-9 (audio)

Scripture quotations are from the ESV® Bible (The Holy Bible, English Standard Version®), © 2001 by Crossway, a publishing ministry of Good News Publishers. Used by permission. All rights reserved.

Cover Design by German Creative

Dedication

To my four, precious daughters.
You are God's greatest treasures to me this side of heaven.

May God bless you with husbands who are moral and Godly,
and will love, honor, and cherish you like Jesus in every way.

I pray the men you inevitably choose to marry, Lord-willing,
heed the warnings and wisdom of this devotional.

Contents

	Preface	7
	Introduction	9
Day-1	Avoid: ISOLATION	13
Day-2	Learn: RELATIONSHIP	17
Day-3	Avoid: REPUTATION	21
Day-4	Learn: VULNERABILITY	25
Day-5	Avoid: PRIDE	29
Day-6	Learn: HUMILITY	33
Day-7	Avoid: IDOLATRY	37
Day-8	Learn: SELF-CONTROL	41
Day-9	Avoid: FEAR	45
Day-10	Learn: COURAGE	49
Day-11	Avoid: DECEPTION	53
Day-12	Learn: HONESTY	57
Day-13	Avoid: MANIPULATION	61
Day-14	Learn: TRUST	65
Day-15	Avoid: LAZINESS	69
Day-16	Learn: PURPOSE	73
Day-17	Avoid: COMPLAINING	77
Day-18	Learn: CONTENTMENT	81
Day-19	Avoid: ARROGANCE	85
Day-20	Learn: MEEKNESS	89

Day-21	Avoid: DENIAL	93
Day-22	Learn: OWNERSHIP	97
Day-23	Avoid: INSECURITY	101
Day-24	Learn: PROTECTION	105
Day-25	Avoid: CALLOUSNESS	109
Day-26	Learn: COMPASSION	113
Day-27	Avoid: ANGER	117
Day-28	Learn: PEACE	121
Day-29	Avoid: VENGEANCE	125
Day-30	Learn: MOURNING	129
Day-31	Avoid: GREED	133
Day-32	Learn: GENEROSITY	137
Day-33	Avoid: DEVIATION	141
Day-34	Learn: ACCOUNTABILITY	145
Day-35	Avoid: WORRY	149
Day-36	Learn: PATIENCE	153
Day-37	Avoid: DESPAIR	157
Day-38	Learn: BROKENNESS	161
Day-39	Avoid: INDIFFERENCE	165
Day-40	Learn: LEADERSHIP	169
	Postface	173
	Author	177

PREFACE

The Road Less Traveled

This devotional has been incredibly humbling to compose. Reason being, I wanted to provide men with a resource they could easily read that was relevant and applicable. It had to identify real problems but offer practical solutions. Therefore, this book compares twenty attributes we must avoid with twenty attributes we should learn instead. The challenge was that I did not want you, the reader, to step outside your comfort zone and get brutally honest with yourself if I was unwilling to do the same. Therefore, this devotional details my personal failures to help model the depth and breadth of vulnerability required to become a man of Godly character.

Reflecting upon my life throughout this process and owning my sins has been painfully difficult, but I thank God for the opportunity to humble myself and expose my foolishness. Self-reflection is paramount to recognizing the error of our ways and how enslaved we are to sin and temptation. No man wants to admit he has chosen poorly in his past or even in his present, but failure provides ample opportunity for us to learn from our choices. Therefore, I pray that by providing a glimpse into my struggles and the hard lessons God has taught me, you will avoid foolishness and discern for yourself the path of righteousness in the absolute truth of God's Word.

As men, we love to fix things. There is something within us which beams with pride when we solve a problem. Yet when it comes to our faith, we cannot fix our sin issues without the Lord's wisdom and strength. Granted, He requires us to make a conscious effort to discipline ourselves with hard work and dedication. Therefore, these next forty days will not be easy. The attributes we will study will be a daily gut-punch as we peel back the layers of our hearts like an onion and shed tears over sins we have committed. Yet with repentance comes forgiveness, which is the pearl of great prize we covet at the conclusion of this forty-day journey.

Fortunately, we have a Savior who took upon Himself the wrath our sins deserve to free us from the chains of bondage. Therefore, as we reconcile in our hearts how far we have fallen from grace, we must never lose sight of the cross of Calvary and the empty tomb which gives us hope and eternal assurance. Our Father in heaven has no desire to watch us perish in misery and suffering. He longs to see us come to saving faith through genuine repentance, but He will not force our hand. Rather, He waits patiently for us to come to our senses and choose for ourselves whom we will ultimately serve.

The bottom-line is that change will never happen if we are unwilling to own our sins. Therefore, I pray we are inspired to face our fears and experience the joy of salvation which comes through Biblical repentance. Keep in mind, self-recognition is critical to restoration and redemption. However, we cannot be spiritually blind to our own blindness and walk around acting as if we can clearly see. That is why we must take a leap of faith and accept discomfort as a golden opportunity to get honest with ourselves. Also, we must wholeheartedly own our sins and the consequences of our actions if we expect to see positive change come to fruition. Only then will we demonstrate the righteous attributes of a Godly man to the glory of Jesus' name.

INTRODUCTION
The Wilderness Journey

If there is one thing the Lord has taught me throughout my life, it is that transformation is impossible without brokenness over sin. As a husband and father who desperately longs to be a man of moral character and integrity, knowing which sins I need to eliminate from my life is just as important as knowing what I should be doing instead. For if I do not know where I am going or what my end goal should be, I will easily lose my way amid spiritual warfare with little chance of survival.

Embarking on a journey deep into the wilderness can be daunting. We must be well-prepared and know the resources we have at our disposal. However, even the greatest survival experts will admit that no one can predict what lies ahead until we have taken a leap of faith and allowed ourselves to be tested beyond our perceived limits. Self-discovery is not for the faint of heart, but it often draws us like a moth to a flame because we want to see if we are capable of surviving the elements. We may feel invincible, but we will never know if that is indeed true until we allow ourselves to be pushed to the brink.

While we may not have the time, energy, or resources to test our limits physically, we face a spiritual wilderness every day of our lives. With unrelenting ferocity, temptation wages war on our psyche and pushes us to the brink of destruction. How then should we respond? Are we to give up, or does God have us precisely where

He wants us when we journey the road less traveled with nothing but our faith in Jesus to protect us?

Spiritual survival is 100% dependent upon Christ because we cannot defeat the enemy by ourselves. Only Jesus' blood which cleanses us from all unrighteousness is powerful enough to save us. Therefore, we must humble ourselves and repent of our sins to have any shot at surviving forty-days in the grueling wilderness of our minds. From there, personal responsibility and accountability must become the bedrock on which we build our foundation of Godly character.

That may require us to perform spiritual amputation in our lives and put an immediate end to particular people, places, and things which tempt us to sin (Matt. 5:29-30). However, if we love God more than false idols, which leave us parched and empty, why would implementing spiritual disciplines to grow our faith not be a wise decision? We can hope our lives would change for the better, but unless we are willing to overhaul our personal behavior, true transformation will never happen.

It is critical we implement non-negotiable, zero-tolerance boundaries to guard our hearts from yielding to temptation and sin. That is the essence of Biblical repentance—turning away from sin and walking by faith in surrender to Christ's authority, obedience to His Word, and submission to His sovereign will. Far too often we believe we can quickly fix our problems and be just fine, but that is like needing a heart transplant and expecting a band-aid to suffice. Rather, what we need is for God to surgically remove the darkness from our hearts and give us new life in Christ.

Granted, it will require radical self-examination and getting much more intimate with the depths of our depravity than we realize. In most cases, we are too scared to embrace that level of vulnerability. However, there is no alternative way to lift ourselves up from the ashes than by facing our fears and bowing reverently before the judgment seat of Christ. **"The sacrifices of God are a broken spirit; a broken and contrite heart, O God, you will not despise" (Psalm 51:17)**.

King David understood that the only way to become a man after God's own heart was to swallow his pride and humble himself. When Nathan the prophet confronted him and held him accountable to God's law, David crumbled spiritually. For the first time, he saw the reality of his sins from God's holy and righteous perspective and knew judgment was upon him. That is why David accepted the consequences of his actions because there was no use making excuses. He chose to sin against the Lord and needed to be held accountable to the wake of destruction his sins created.

David's example is a great reminder that minimizing or justifying sin is futile. If we want to make positive changes in our lives, we must accept full responsibility for the decisions we make to please ourselves rather than God. Recognition is key but it cannot stop there, because knowing we are sinners and making the necessary changes to turn away from sinning again are two completely different issues. We may possess the best intentions in the world to change, but without a plan of action to remedy our problems, we will continue to make the same poor choices time and again.

In the end, God will do what only He can do and perform a miracle in our hearts if we are committed to change, but we must walk by faith and allow His Spirit to radically transform our hearts from the inside-out. Conviction is a powerful tool God uses to remove the cancer of sin from our lives, but we must give the Spirit free reign to leave no stone unturned. Only then will we begin to demonstrate the character attributes of a Godly man which will change the trajectory of our lives and give us confidence to survive forty days in the wilderness.

Bottom-line, until we are sick and tired of being sick and tired, we will never overcome the chains of bondage which leave us enslaved to sin. If we have not hit rock bottom, we still have room to fall before understanding why we need Jesus so desperately. A man who is unwilling to admit how selfish and wretched he truly is will never taste the joy of freedom from sin. He cannot because he has not developed enough hatred for his sin to ultimately change his wicked behavior.

Truly, heart change will only come when we weep and mourn over our sins, which requires us to view our thoughts and actions from God's holy perspective. Thankfully, He has given us His Word to provide a roadmap to redemption and restoration, but we must stick to the trail and not veer off course assuming there is a shortcut to reconciliation with the Father. If we have any desire to rise up from the ashes and turn away from sin once and for all, we must surrender our pride and run to Christ. Otherwise, we are just fooling ourselves.

The Father's arms are open wide and ready to embrace us, but first, we must recognize the error of our ways and repent of our sins. If we do, we will find it easier to walk the road less traveled and survive the next forty-days in the wilderness. This journey toward godliness may be the turning point in our lives, but we must display vulnerability. God is plenty capable of performing a miracle in our hearts, but we must cast off the scarlet letter of guilt, shame, and regret for transformation to occur. For in Christ alone, all things are possible (Matt. 19:26).

Day 1 – Isolation

> *"Whoever isolates himself seeks his own desire;*
> *he breaks out against all sound judgment."*
>
> — Proverbs 18:1 —

Men are prone to isolate themselves. That fact is undeniable. The problem is the more we isolate from accountability and the wise counsel of others, the more vulnerable we are to the evil schemes of the enemy. Isolation has always been Satan's most effective strategy of attack since the Garden of Eden when Eve was alone and tempted to eat the forbidden fruit. She had no reason to disobey God's Word. Yet in that moment, she fell victim to deceit. Therefore, we must learn from her mistake. For when accountability is lacking, there is no one to speak truth to our minds before we yield to fleshly desires which will haunt us forever.

Scripture warns, **"Be sober-minded; be watchful. Your adversary the devil prowls around like a roaring lion, seeking someone to devour" (1 Peter 5:8)**. Isolation is strategically intended by our enemy to expose our weaknesses. Separation from the protection of the body of Christ is a recipe for disaster. It makes us think we require no help from those who love and care about us. It also baits us into believing we are the only ones who can ultimately be trusted. We have the ability to convince ourselves practically any behavior is acceptable if wise counsel and discernment are lacking, because self-gratification only fuels our efforts to rationalize and justify our sins.

I wish I could say this was all foreign to me, but I know the danger of isolation all too well. At an early age, I was exposed to pornography. Unfortunately, that seed of lustful desire took root in my mind and flourished over time. The more images I consumed, the more addicted I became to sin. It only enslaved my heart and mind further because I kept it a secret. What I learned over time was that sexual desire can never be satisfied. Its craving is insatiable because it desires more fuel to keep the fire burning. Unfortunately, I allowed my mind to become discontent where I sacrificed marital happiness to feed my flesh. I took risks I never thought possible to quench a selfish appetite which never could be satisfied.

I also learned that pornography fuels self-gratification which provides a man the opportunity to satisfy his sexual desire in the seclusion and privacy of his home. However, pornography and masturbation are not merely a single man's battle. Married men are just as addicted to lusts of the flesh. However, the risks associated carry far greater weight because the consequences of actions are more severe. That is why adultery is considered the most destructive sin a marriage can encounter, and one of the two justifiable reasons God allows for divorce, if necessary.

The problem with pornography (or any other sin addiction) is its unique dependency on isolation which enables us to act out on our passions. Gone are the days when venturing outside the home was required to satisfy our guilty desires. The internet provides everything we need to appease our flesh at the push of a button. Anything we want can be delivered to our screen, inbox, or door with relative ease and comfort for immediate satisfaction. All we need is a computer, tablet, or smartphone, and the pleasures of this world are easily at our fingertips and ready for consumption while devoid of accountability.

When I think about all the years I wasted feeding my lustful addiction, I am appalled by my selfishness. Not only did I struggle with pornography as a bachelor, but I secretly brought sin into our marriage as well. Rather than change my isolation tendencies and seek Biblical counseling to earn victory over my addiction, I compartmentalized my temptations as manageable to avoid asking for help. The problem was that accountability was non-existent in my life, and I had no voice of reason to expose my poor judgment and hold me accountable to zero-tolerance boundaries to protect my marriage. I had bought into the lie that I could only count on myself, so I hid my addiction rather than owning and exposing my sins, inevitably destroying my marriage in the process.

Before Jesus began His ministry journey, the Spirit led Him into the wilderness for forty days and forty nights while He fasted and prayed. However, just because Jesus was doing a good thing by clearing His mind and tuning His heart to the Father's voice does not mean He lacked opposition. Clearly, the enemy was ready to attack! Satan preyed upon Jesus' lack of physical nourishment as a means of tempting Him to abandon His mission. Therefore, we should not be surprised when Satan uses the same tactic to attack us when we are tired, weary, and vulnerable to isolation.

On the whole, isolation is an area we are wise to avoid except in the confines of prayer. There are no benefits to avoiding personal relationships which protect our hearts and guard our minds from sin and temptation. That is why accountability is so valuable in the life of a Christ-follower. It allows others to speak truth into the darkness of our minds and draw us into the light of God's grace where true healing is found. However, the choice is ours, which means if we truly want to change our behavior, we must stop isolating ourselves.

Application

1. Why is isolation Satan's #1 strategy of attack?
2. When are you most prone to isolate from others?
3. What patterns of behavior promote isolation in your life?
4. Why is accountability critical to overcoming your tendency to isolate from others?
5. How has isolation provided a favorable environment for you to satisfy and feed your fleshly desires?
6. What risks are you taking when you hide your sins rather than confess to those who can counsel you?
7. What has God taught you about the dangers of isolation?
8. How can you invest into healthy relationships which will protect your heart and mind?

Prayer

Lord, thank You for loving me when I continue to isolate myself. I confess that I have become dangerously prone to living in darkness rather than the light of truth. Instill in me an insatiable hunger to read my Bible and apply what it says. I desperately need accountability but often do not know where to turn for help. Give me boldness and courage to step outside my comfort zone, humble myself, and seek counsel when intervention is needed. Your wisdom is critical to my survival. Therefore, help me seek healthy relationships within the body of Christ to sharpen my character, hold me accountable, and honor You most of all. Amen.

Day 2 – Relationship

> *"Then the LORD God formed the man of dust from the ground and breathed into his nostrils the breath of life, and the man became a living creature."*
>
> — Genesis 2:7 —

The true mark of a Godly man begins and ends with recognizing who he is in the grand scheme of creation. What a man believes about God and his relationship to Him is critical to understanding personal identity. It reveals a man's purpose and explains why God created him in the first place. That may not seem like such a big deal, but God formed man from the dust of the earth and breathed life into his nostrils for the sole purpose of relational intimacy. Therefore, if we desire to be righteous men of Godly character, we must understand why relationships are the foundation of our connection to the Lord and one another.

Companionship is paramount in our culture today. Even though men tend to isolate themselves for various reasons, no man truly desires to be alone. If we have watched the History Channel's popular survival competition, "Alone," we would quickly discover that lack of human companionship is the #1 reason contestants tap out and go home. Though they may be able to endure the harsh elements, they cannot seem to survive not having someone to talk with or share personal experiences. In many ways, that revelation is a shock to their systems, even though they know beforehand how the game works. They simply cannot seem to fathom how unbearable the lack of relational intimacy will be until they are left all alone to survive.

From the beginning, God knew that it was not good for a man to live alone. Though He created Adam in His own image, God realized that he lacked a suitable companion. So while Adam slept, God took out one of his ribs and created woman (Gen. 2:18-23). God's decision is such an incredible picture of what self-sacrifice looks like in marriage—giving of oneself for another. Adam did not know it at the time, but the rib he sacrificed provided more blessing than he ever imagined. From that moment on, he not only had vertical intimacy with God but horizontal intimacy with his wife in an entirely new way.

Recently, God taught me a hard lesson on the fragility of life and how quickly it can vanish. On November 6, 2022, at the age of 44, I had a massive heart attack. Unbeknownst to me, due to bad family genes, my LAD (widow-maker) artery was 70% blocked. I needed immediate surgery to install a heart stent and keep the valve open to allow blood to flow freely while medications worked to dissipate the clot which had formed. Thankfully, my surgery was successful, but it was a huge wake up call to me, my wife, Amber, and our four daughters. Life could have turned out much differently had God chosen to take me home far earlier than we expected.

It is sobering to consider how my family would have suffered had I not taken my symptoms seriously. What if I had not sought immediate medical attention when I felt all the warnings signs of a heart attack? What if I had been stubborn and tried to tough it out by grinding through the pain and discomfort? I likely would not have survived. Honestly, the only thing which scared me in that moment was leaving Amber a widow and my daughters fatherless. I was not scared to die because I knew my salvation was secure.

However, it was the lack of relationship and spiritual intimacy my death would have caused my family which consumed my focus. I wanted to live so I could experience all the joys and trials of life with them. Quality time with my wife and daughters was all that mattered when life suddenly flashed before my eyes, because they mean the world to me.

If we stop and consider the relationships we keep, some are good and healthy while others pale in comparison. Regardless, God has ordained the families we are in for a reason. He has given us wives and children for a reason. He has guided our paths to live in our respective locations for a reason. He has brought people into our lives to pour into us for a reason. He has allowed us to endure trials and hardships for a reason. He has even remained patient when we have gone astray and distanced ourselves from Him. There are no accidents in divine creation because God is sovereign and has a purpose for every situation we encounter, which means He works things for our good by drawing us into relationship with His Son.

Therefore, rather than examining our lives from a glass-half-empty perspective, let us embrace the seasons of life we find ourselves in and appreciate those whom God has crossed our paths. For quality time together with those we love is a precious commodity and we are wise to treasure that gift. Some would even consider it priceless, especially if they have lost a loved one unexpectedly. Therefore, we should utilize the time we have been given and not take a single day for granted. We should also express to those we love how much they mean to us. The future is not guaranteed. We can be here today and gone tomorrow. However, where we are headed eternally is something we must reconcile today rather than waiting.

Application

1. What is required to maintain healthy relationships?
2. What changes can you make to spend more time with God?
3. How can you strategically invest time developing personal relationships which honor your faith in Christ?
4. Why do you believe God put you in your respective family?
5. How have you seen God bring people into your life for a season rather than a lifetime?
6. If tomorrow is not guaranteed, how can you live each day as if it was your last? What changes could you make?
7. Who are the most important people in your life? How can you better express your love and appreciation to them?

Prayer

Lord, thank You for creating me and providing abundant opportunity to have a personal relationship with You. I do not appreciate the priceless gift of your love to me. Oftentimes, I get so focused on myself that I forget to spend quality time talking to You and reading Your Word daily. Teach me to be a more disciplined man who prioritizes a personal relationship with You most of all. Help me appreciate the family You have given me. I no longer want to complain about their failures and shortcomings. I often fail to tell my family and friends what they mean to me, but I know I need to because tomorrow is not guaranteed. Therefore, let me use the precious time You have given to bless others and share Your Word. Amen.

Day 3 - Reputation

"A good name is better than precious ointment."

— *Ecclesiastes 7:1* —

What is a man without his reputation to precede him? How can others know if he is moral and righteous without evidence of his good works? The answer lies in the wisdom of King Solomon who pointed to a man's name as the means by which his personal reputation is revealed and true character defined. Names have meaning based on personal history. They give others an indication of what to expect from our behavior based on what they know about us. The challenge is a name can mean different things to different people, especially when our public and private personas contradict one another.

Often, we fail to see how personal behavior inconsistencies add or detract from the reputation we work so hard to portray. For instance, we can look in the mirror and feel as if we are the same person publicly as we are privately. However, truth be told, we often live double lives to hide our failures and protect our insecurities. We think, "If others really knew what I struggle with behind closed doors, they would reject me and walk away." As a result, we often wear masks to maintain a false self-image rather than lowering our guard so others can see who we truly are.

I know the deception game all too well because I once manipulated my reputation to portray myself publicly as a strong, spiritual leader, even though I lived to appease my flesh privately. I was consumed with lust and compartmentalized my sin as independent from the rest of my life, so much that I rejected the notion that my private choices impacted others. I knew yielding to fleshly desires was wrong. I just did not want to change my behavior or make amends for the poor decisions I had made through the years. Consequently, I covered my sins to maintain a righteous identity publicly instead of owning the consequences of my actions.

Hypocrisy can actually hijack our reputation because it baits us into thinking we need to hide our sins to maintain a more favorable public image. This is an area where the enemy can prey upon our fear of failure. However, living in the shadows has no power to release us from the bondage of sin. It only enslaves us deeper into darkness and the pleasures of this world. That is why we must choose a different path by building a reputation which points to God's authority in our lives. Failure to do so only feeds our flesh and draws us farther away from Christ.

Heart change begins with asking ourselves, "Who am I, who do I serve, and to whom do I belong?" It all helps to determine whose voice reigns supreme in our lives, because personal reputation has the power to point people to Christ. However, it can also draw unbelievers away from the Christian faith we profess if we are living for ourselves. Therefore, we must lay down our pride and allow Jesus full access to our hearts. Keep in mind, the enemy would have us believe we can build a name for ourselves while serving God at the same time. However, that is a lie. We cannot serve two masters, which means we must choose whether God's reputation means more to us.

Jesus said, **"No one can serve two masters, for either he will hate the one and love the other, or he will be devoted to the one and despise the other. You cannot serve God and money"**

(Matthew 6:24). He also echoed the same sentiment in Luke 14:28 when He cautioned His followers to count the cost before surrendering their lives to follow Him. Oftentimes, living for righteousness can be incredibly difficult. It requires us to stand boldly for truth and resist temptation and peer pressure. However, what does it say about us if we are willing to compromise our faith to protect our self-image?

Regrettably, I spent more time protecting my personal reputation than changing my behavior. For years, I failed to see how hypocrisy impacted my family. Rather than humbling myself before the Lord and repenting of my sins, I chose to plunge deeper into my lustful addiction until God intervened and saved me from bondage. He allowed me to wallow in the pit of guilt, shame, and regret, so I could see the error of my ways and embrace His grace and mercy. In retrospect, God saved my life by giving me exactly what I foolishly desired, and I am a better man today because He crushed my pride and exposed the hypocritical mask I had been wearing. He allowed me to see my sins for what they had become—spiritual death.

We often forget that God is far more concerned about the glory of His name than protecting our personal reputation. Therefore, He will ensure we have ample opportunity to recognize the error of our ways and make amends for our sins. It all comes down to whether we truly belong to His family, which requires us to repent of our sins and accept Jesus as Lord and Savior. In the end, God is patiently waiting with open arms to welcome us home and receive us into His kingdom, but we must choose between life or death. If life, we must humble ourselves, repent of our sins, and turn from our wicked ways. Only then will we truly be free from the bondage of sin. If death, then we are merely living for the pleasures of this world and will ultimately reap the consequences of our rebellion.

Application

1. How would you define your personal reputation? Who are you as a man?
2. Does your reputation reflect more about you or God?
3. What difference does it make if your reputation changes based on your environment or the company you keep?
4. How have you been baited into wearing a self-protecting mask to hide your personal failures and insecurities?
5. Which sins do you hold close to your heart that no one other than God knows about?
6. How aware are others of your personal faith in Christ?
7. How can you begin reflecting the image of Christ rather than your own self-image?

Prayer

Lord, I have been so focused on making a name for myself that I have forgotten how my life should reflect Your name above all. Please forgive me. I recognize how much I have hidden my sins to protect my reputation so others would think highly of me. I have been far more consumed with the pleasures of this world than I should. I have also ignored what You have taught me through Your Word. Help me become the same man of righteousness in public as in private so that my thoughts and behavior avoid hypocrisy. I want to reflect Your grace, mercy, and love so that Your name is glorified, not mine. Break me of my pride and help me to clearly see the error of my selfish ways. Amen.

Day 4 - Vulnerability

"Therefore, confess your sins to one another and pray for one another, that you may be healed. The prayer of a righteous person has great power as it is working."

— James 5:16 —

In the world of testosterone, vulnerability is similar to the plague. Men avoid it at all cost because the risks associated are practically immeasurable. The problem with vulnerability is that we do not know what to expect. If we share too little, people will not know who we are. If we share too much, people might distance themselves from spending time with us. As a result, we often aim for the status quo and land somewhere in the middle, which is called transparency. It is not that we are unwilling to let others into our personal lives. We just want to maintain control over information being shared in whatever context and environment we feel comfortable.

Truthfully, most men aim for being transparent rather than vulnerable. It is all based on presumed safety vs. calculated risks. Think of it like playing poker. Transparency calculates our bets proportionately so we do not fall in the red, whereas vulnerability calls our bluff and goes all-in, risking everything, come what may. It may seem like they are the same thing, but nothing could be further from the truth because transparency shares who we are to the extent we feel comfortable. It is risky but also measured to ensure we retain control over perceived outcomes. On the contrary, vulnerability throws all caution to the wind and compels us to reach into the depths of depravity. In turn, we share our personal stories, no matter how dark and painful they may be, with the intention of glorifying God through our trials and the lessons we learned.

In groups I have led through my **"Wilderness Survival"** discipleship curriculum, I have discovered that most men will never experience the immeasurable freedom which comes with vulnerability until it is modeled. That is why I always take the lead and share about my personal failures to demonstrate how a man must be willing to take a risk to achieve godliness. For example, I would prefer not to talk about my former addiction to lust and porn, but I also know the majority of men have struggled with the same issue because sexual temptation targets us constantly. Most guys are too afraid to talk about their sexual sins because it is embarrassing. However, if I am willing to humble myself and confess my sins, others know that airing their dirty laundry is safe. In turn, they usually take a risk and open up about their struggles as well.

There is nothing more powerful than being in fellowship with men who are broken by God and willingly confess their darkest sins to one another. An eight-hundred-pound gorilla is lifted off our shoulders when we share our personal struggles and praise God for saving us from complete ruin. Confession allows us to experience freedom from the bondage of guilt, shame, and regret, and sets our course on rehabilitation and restoration. Repentance is the first step, but once we begin that journey, God will use our testimonies for His glory, because He meets us in our moments of vulnerability and heals the wounds deep within our souls.

What may worry us before we share our testimonies is a distant memory the moment our private truth becomes public. We realize that confession is an act of worship to Christ who sets us free from sin. That is often what we fail to comprehend about vulnerability. It is not about glorifying ourselves, our stories, or what we did to change, but what God did in and through us to promote ownership, personal responsibility, and accountability for our sins. God is glorified when we share our stories of redemption, and vulnerability gives context to the reasons why we are so thankful for His amazing grace.

I will be the first to admit that Biblical counseling saved my marriage. When I confessed the depth and breadth of my sexual immorality to Amber, we immediately embarked upon seven months of marital counseling because we were on the brink of divorce. I had betrayed her trust in ways I will never fully comprehend, enough to make her question whether she could ever live with me again. She had every right to divorce me because she did not deserve the weight of spiritual warfare I had thrust upon her. My confession crushed her psyche and plunged her into a season of mourning and depression. It is a season of our marriage I deeply regret. Nonetheless, that is where our story of marital redemption began many years ago.

God did a miracle in both our hearts—for me to change and for her to forgive—and our marriage stands today as a humble testament to forgiveness and mercy. Granted, it is not easy to talk about. It tempts me to question whether I should share our story at all because of the pain I caused and how I completely disregarded my marriage vows. However, our story (which Amber allows me to share) magnifies Christ who died for my sins and gave my wife the courage and strength to forgive. Embracing vulnerability is all about glorifying Christ so others will take a risk and experience the freedom which comes with sharing personal testimonies.

Application

1. Why is transparency safe and vulnerability risky?
2. Have you ever given your personal faith testimony? What details could you share? Which should you keep private?
3. How have you leaned toward transparency vs. vulnerability with those in your life?
4. What fears or insecurities hinder you from being vulnerable with your family and friends?
5. Have you ever confessed your darkest sins to others? If not, why? If so, what freedom did you experience?
6. If your story of personal salvation and redemption from sin ultimately glorifies God, why would you not share it?
7. How has God ministered to you in the valley of despair?

Prayer

Lord, You have blessed me beyond measure and saved my soul from hell. Thank You for suffering a criminal's death on my behalf and freeing me from sin. I confess that fear of man often silences my voice from sharing Your Gospel of salvation. Sometimes, I just take the safer route and share about Your grace without giving the full background and context of how You saved my soul from ruin. Help me step outside my comfort zone and embrace vulnerability. I no longer want to hide in the dark shadows, for You have shown immeasurable grace and mercy when I least deserved it. Please give me courage to share my testimony publicly so that others may come to know You and find salvation in Christ. Amen.

Day 5 - Pride

*"Pride goes before destruction,
and a haughty spirit before a fall."*

— *Proverbs 16:18* —

Is it possible to work on becoming men of Godly character and not talk about selfish pride which wages war upon our souls? Pride drove Satan to declare mutiny against the heavenly hosts and it is the dominant issue we face today when we assume we know better than God. It fuels our fleshly desires and tempts us to abandon the safety and security of His presence for the pleasures of this world. No man is exempt from falling victim to pride because we are all sinners and choose daily to disobey the Lord's commands. Therefore, pride should be a continual focus of our attention if we desire to be men of righteousness.

What does pride actually look like? There are some instances when pride is not inherently evil but intended for good. For instance, we can be proud of our children when they use proper manners, obey instructions, and respect authority. However, pride hinders more than it helps in most cases, which means we must discern how to avoid its deadly snare. Noah Webster's 1828 Dictionary provides great clarity because it defines pride as "inordinate self-esteem; an unreasonable conceit of one's own superiority in talents, beauty, wealth, accomplishments, rank, or elevation in office, which manifests itself in lofty airs, distance, reserve, and often in contempt of others." In other words, pride is the exaltation of oneself at the expense of God and others.

In a world where professional athletes, movie stars, and musicians are idolized for their accomplishments, it is easy for people to glorify themselves and presume self-exaltation is mandatory for success. The more they point to the one in the mirror as the source of their strength, the more they distance themselves from the truth of God's Word which can save their souls. Scripture warns, **"Everyone who is arrogant in heart is an abomination to the Lord; be assured, he will not go unpunished" (Proverbs 16:5)**. Consequently, we are wise to check our pride at the door and ensure our posture before the Lord is reverent and humble. Thus, if we expect to avoid being cast into hell on judgment day because we are guilty of sin, we must repent of our pride and humble ourselves accordingly.

As the youngest of five children, I remember feeling the need to prove myself as a man growing up. Even though my siblings never held anything over my head, I still had a chip on my shoulder bent on proving my worth. I was determined to exceed their accomplishments because I wanted notoriety. I was foolish and competitive and my brothers were my role models growing up, so it made sense for me to compare myself to them in every way. Whether they were great athletes, successful in sales, comfortable in public speaking, or skilled in performing arts, I wanted to prove I was just as good as they were and make a name for myself just like they did.

Fortunately, God blessed me despite my foolish pride. Though I knew He gave me skills and talents to achieve my goals, I foolishly took credit for what He did in and through me. Looking back, I am ashamed of arrogantly assuming that all the blessings I received from God had anything to do with me. I was a self-proclaimed Christian but knew little to nothing about the Bible, and my naïve pride proved I had much to learn about humility and dying to love of self. Though I attempted to present myself as a God-honoring man publicly, I took credit for what God did in my life behind closed doors. It was not until I began reading Scripture that the Lord exposed my arrogance and convicted me of my sins. Only then did change begin to take place in my selfish heart.

Oftentimes, we believe we are giving God all the credit for what He has done in our lives when, in actuality, we are sharing the limelight instead. Many of us struggle to praise God for our success. We know that we need to glorify God, but our words and actions paint conflicting pictures. A good litmus test to gauge our spiritual maturity is based on how we view personal income. For example, do we consider employment earnings as God's resources or ours? If God's, then tithing 10% of our income should not cause us to flinch in any way. For if all belongs to God, we are stewards of His resources, not ours. Therefore, giving should be the easiest thing we do in life.

However, do we truly believe everything we own belongs to Him? God only requires a tithe of 10%, yet the vast majority of Christians fail to maintain that simple standard. When we view things from the lens of stewardship vs. ownership, money begins to expose how prideful we have become when we believe our income belongs to us. However, would we rather have 90% of our income with God or 100% without Him? Even though everything we own belongs to Him, tithing feels like an enormous sacrifice. Yet if we would trust Him at His Word and surrender our pride, we would quickly realize that His blessings are immeasurable when we give more than what He expects from us (Mal. 3:8-10).

Application

1. Would you consider yourself prideful? Why or why not?
2. What holds you back from allowing your family and friends to expose prideful tendencies they see in your behavior?
3. Where is the distinguishing line in the sand between sinful pride and righteousness?
4. Who can hold you accountable when your attitude starts to become prideful rather than humble?
5. What consequences have you endured because of prideful arrogance?
6. How has God broken your personal will and humbled you with spiritual discipline?
7. Do you believe everything you own belongs to God? Why?

Prayer

Lord, it is convicting to think about how easily I have surrendered to sinful pride throughout my life. I often feel like Paul when he said, **"For I do not do the good I want, but the evil I do not want is what I keep on doing" (Romans 7:19)**. Selfish pride has made a complete mess of my life and the consequences of my actions still haunt me to this day. However, I know Your grace is sufficient despite my failures. Help me die to love of self and display humility by not taking credit for Your countless blessings. All I am and all I have is because of Your grace and mercy. I never again want to steal Your glory for selfish gain, for You are worthy to be honored and praised forevermore. Amen.

Day 6 - Humility

> *"Therefore, humble yourselves under the mighty hand of God so that at the proper time he may exalt you."*
>
> — 1 Peter 5:6 —

Nowhere in Scripture are we taught to go and be humble. Rather, we are instructed to seek opportunities where we can intentionally humble ourselves by swallowing our pride and setting aside personal comforts. Humility requires action because it is a badge of honor we earn through self-sacrifice. By putting the needs of others before our own, we die to love of self and cast insecurities aside as we shine the light of Christ to others. However, pride can hinder us from stepping outside our comfort zone, especially when it comes to owning our sins and making amends for damages we have caused.

There are many instances throughout my life where God has allowed me to wallow in the filth and depravity of my sins so I could experience the gift of humility. For example, one day I was raking up yard debris and needed somewhere to quickly dispose of it. Our trash service does not accept yard waste, so I decided to dispose of it in our neighbor's dumpster down the street without their permission. Where I grew up, a residential dumpster is fair game. Needless to say, an upset homeowner came knocking at my door the next evening eager to confront my selfish decision and give me a stern piece of her mind.

In that moment, the problem I faced was that not only did I sin against my neighbor, but I also had my oldest daughter help me dump the trash as well. My foolishness cast a wider net than I first realized, and I was forced to own my sins and accept whatever consequences my neighbor deemed necessary to atone for it. I certainly apologized for my actions at the time. However, I also knew that saying, "I'm sorry!" when confronted was not adequate. I had to swallow my pride and humble myself by stepping outside my comfort zone, meeting her husband at their home as well, and asking him face-to-face to please forgive me for taking advantage of his personal property without permission.

Humility is all about embracing a reverent posture before God, owning our sins, and making amends with those we have sinned against. Looking back, I could have easily reconciled that apologizing for my sins was good enough, but God would not allow me to reconcile the guilt, shame, and regret I felt in my heart. I had to go the extra mile. I also knew that I needed to set a better example as the spiritual leader in my home, which meant making the necessary effort to repent of my sins and reconcile with those I had sinned against, regardless of how uncomfortable and humiliating it made me feel.

Oftentimes, we fail to see the importance of humbling ourselves before God and reconciling sins we have committed against our neighbors. It is relatively easy to offer halfhearted apologies which merely communicate, "I'm sorry for getting caught," rather than, "I recognize the error of my ways and accept the consequences of my actions." However, asking others to forgive us empowers them to play judge and jury on our behalf. It means we give them a choice to make, instead of us making a reluctant act of contrition and walking away callous or indifferent towards their reaction or response.

Humbling ourselves does not always have to be about owning our sins. We can also put ourselves in positions where we accept the role of a servant and selflessly meet the needs of others who may have nowhere else to turn for help. The key is ensuring our heart's motivation is selfless and pure. God has given us far more than we could ask for or imagine, but He can also remove all He has graciously given if we are hoarding blessings for ourselves. Therefore, it should be our joy and privilege to share the gifts we have received from God to bless others by investing our time, energy, and resources helping those who are in need.

Practicing humility far outweighs the moments where God is forced to step in and hold us accountable for sins we commit against Him. Therefore, we must step outside our comfort zone and love others like Jesus would. However, if our attitudes are self-serving, we are not shining the light of Christ but merely glorifying ourselves and demonstrating how truly prideful we are. We may not realize how important motivation is to learning humility, but if our hearts are not in the right place, we will miss out on opportunities to grow our faith and glorify God in the process.

May we never forget that even though God has the power to crush us, He chooses to love us by disciplining our behavior when we need a heavy dose of humility to grab our attention. That is how great the Father's love is when we least deserve it, and we are wise to praise Him endlessly for the gift of salvation He freely provides. Jesus did not have to accept the role of a servant to die for our sins, but He submitted to the Father's will and set aside His personal comforts, doing for us what we could not do for ourselves. He humbled Himself and died for our sins, and we are called to do the same so we can share His immeasurable love with others.

Application

1. Would you consider yourself humble? Why or why not?
2. Is it easier to humble yourself or be humbled by God?
3. What gifts, talents, or resources has God graciously given you to bless others less fortunate than yourself?
4. Why is busyness a barrier to learning humility?
5. How is humbling yourself before family members different than doing so with friends or even complete strangers?
6. Do you typically say, "I'm sorry!" or ask, "Would you please forgive me?" Why is this distinction significant?
7. How is the fear of man stopping you from seeking ample opportunities to humble yourself?

Prayer

Lord, humility is not something which comes natural to me. I tend to enjoy my personal comforts, but I know that is no excuse for not putting myself in uncomfortable situations to grow my faith. Help me open my eyes and ears to the needs of those around me. Soften my heart and break my pride so I can exemplify a man whose character is defined by humility. Lord, if there is any sin in me that I am holding onto, please break me from it and show me the error of my ways. I do not want pride or arrogance to be a reason my family and friends keep their distance from me. I may not be a righteous man just yet but help me grow in my knowledge and understanding of what humility looks like so I may glorify Your name. Amen.

Day 7 - Idolatry

> *"Do not lay up for yourselves treasures on earth,*
> *where moth and rust destroy and where thieves break in and steal,*
> *but lay up for yourselves treasures in heaven, where neither moth*
> *nor rust destroys and where thieves do not break in and steal.*
> *For where your treasure is, there your heart will be also."*
>
> — Matthew 6:19-21 —

Idolatry is a term we rarely hear referenced in our culture, yet it encompasses far more than pagan worship of images or sculptures. From Scripture's perspective, idolatry stretches beyond man-made works of art and focuses on spiritual worship deep within our hearts. When Jesus spoke these words in His sermon on the mount, He was exposing what we worship. His intent on defining treasure was designed to convict us about people, places, and things which consume our attention and draw us away from quality time with God. Thus, we are wise to take notice and examine our hearts carefully.

The challenge is that some things we desire in life are not necessarily evil, such as sex, money, or even alcohol. However, when they are worshipped and abused for selfish gain or worldly pleasure, we are guilty of idolatry. That is why the first commandment God gave Moses, **"You shall have no other gods before me" (Exodus 20:3)**, is so critical. It candidly addresses what the Lord is most concerned about. He expects our full devotion of heart, mind, body, and soul, because no treasure of this world can compare to the blessing of living for Him and making Jesus Christ our personal Lord and Savior.

When I reflect upon my business career, I believe I have said, "No, thank you!" to promotional opportunities far more than I have declared, "Yes, please!" Reason being, I am unwilling to sacrifice the precious years I have with my family—to watch my girls grow up and be an integral part of their daily lives. I never want to miss an opportunity to spend quality time with them or provide a shoulder to cry on at any moment. Climbing the corporate ladder, being a manager, traveling often, and relocating constantly are sacrifices I am simply unwilling to make. My attitude has always been about contentment with God's provision. Therefore, if I make enough income to clothe my family, put food on the table, and a roof overhead, then I have all I need because God has graciously blessed us beyond measure.

At times, the decision to say, "No!" has resulted in spirited conversations with managers and executives in my company. I have had a blessed career in corporate sales for over two decades and been asked on more than one occasion why I am not at a higher position in our organization. My response is always simple because family and ministry are my top priorities, and I will not sacrifice serving God and my family for a career. For if I pursue a higher rank which requires greater investment of my time, I will miss out on priceless memories with those I love who matter most.

What always strikes me is the reaction I get when I explain why I have chosen to decline promotional opportunities. I could be a Director or Vice President at this point in my career, but I have chosen to remain in sales because my faith and family mean more. Ironically, the response I typically receive begins with, "If I had to do it all over again…" because what people recognize in that brief moment of vulnerability is that life is not about money, power, title, or prestige. It is as if the past flashes before their eyes. They weigh the choices they have made and amount of quality time and family events they have missed. In turn, they begin to see their sacrifices for what they truly are and inevitably regret some of the choices they made pursuing what they assumed were most important.

In the end, all that matters to God is where we place our treasure. For if we believe the pleasures of this world will satisfy our hearts, then we will invest time, energy, and resources pursuing idols at the expense of our faith. Keep in mind, Jesus' intent in Matt. 6:19-21 was not for us to quit our jobs and stay home, because failing to provide for our families is a sin (1 Tim. 5:8). Rather, His message was that we should recalibrate our efforts to what impacts eternity so we are less focused on temporary treasures and more intentional sowing seeds of righteousness which will impact future generations.

One easy way to evaluate how enslaved we are to the things of this world is to consider how we would respond if they were all taken away. For example, if our homes were destroyed due to a tornado, fire, or flood, would we be devastated by the loss of family memories or possessions? If our loved ones suddenly died and we were left all alone, would we struggle finding strength to live again? If anything unfortunate were to happen to us, would we bless God or curse His name? All are difficult questions to answer, but Job endured all these things and still glorified the Lord despite immeasurable suffering (Job 1:21). In the end, we all have choices to make, but discerning who or what is most important in our lives is arguably the greatest decision we will ever make this side of heaven.

Application

1. Are you fearful of unintentionally worshipping idols? Why?
2. Which idols are you prone to gravitate toward when trials of life overwhelm your mind?
3. Would you consider yourself a false worshipper of worldly pleasures? Why or why not?
4. How can things God created which are holy and good be twisted into idols you worship instead?
5. What boundaries can you implement into your daily life to guard your heart against idolatry?
6. How can personal relationships unintentionally become an idol you worship?
7. What treasures can you store up for eternity to bless future generations?

Prayer

Lord, You are the author of all creation. What You have made is good, but sometimes I worship Your creation more than glorifying You. Please forgive me for allowing false idols to distract me from reading Your Word and spending quality time with You in prayer. Please expose the idols which I am holding onto far too much. Help me trust You rather than myself when I am overwhelmed by trials, so that my way of escape is found in You and not the pleasures of this world. Give me wisdom to see my sins for what they truly are and help me discern right from wrong so I do not make the same foolish decisions ever again. Amen.

Day 8 – Self-Control

"A man without self-control is like a city broken into and left without walls."

— *Proverbs 25:28* —

Self-control is arguably the most important tool in our arsenal to quench spiritual warfare. It enables us to cut off temptation before it becomes sin in our lives by utilizing the way of escape God provides to avoid the enemy's attacks. Self-control is basically the Swiss army knife of spiritual disciplines. It works in literally every situation we find ourselves and allows us to apply what Scripture teaches by using discretion and discernment. A man with self-control thinks before he speaks and counts the costs before he acts, enabling him to tap into experiential knowledge and wisdom to make wise decisions.

Conversely, lack of self-control can prove catastrophic. Words that describe such a man are brash, blunt, impulsive, and foolish. Those who lack this discipline are quite dangerous because they think of themselves before they consider the feelings and safety of others. Truly, they can cause great harm if not careful. For instance, the main reason why sin is so rampant in our culture today is because self-control is significantly lacking to protect us from fleshly desires. It began when Adam and Eve ate the forbidden fruit. Since then, we have likewise struggled to control our selfishness which yearns for everything our hearts desire.

Working in corporate sales for so long, I have attended

numerous sales meetings and customer events where alcohol is served. Drinking socially is virtually commonplace, yet I often wonder whether people who call themselves Christians would continue drinking, especially excessively, if they knew others in the room struggled with addiction. Personally, I rarely drink because I am sensitive to my influence on others and what my personal behavior condones. Moreover, I always want to be in control of my actions and alcohol would impair my ability to make wise decisions. Therefore, I abstain out of caution. For me, it all comes down to overconsumption and how easily people can lose their ability to control their behavior when they become intoxicated by alcohol in excess.

Keep in mind, my decision to abstain is intentional across all areas of my life. While I do not believe alcohol is evil, I avoid drinking because I have seen it frequently abused throughout my life. Growing up, I witnessed intoxicated adults get behind the wheel of a car and drive home more times than I care to remember. Those memories of watching friends and family make foolish decisions has shaped who I am today. I am also aware that my reputation as a Christian is a badge of honor I carry with me. Therefore, I want to protect my personal witness to share the Gospel by ensuring that who I am publicly mirrors who I am privately. Moreover, I am a husband and father who is called by God to be a righteous leader in my home. Therefore, my example of self-control is paramount to earn and maintain my family's trust and respect.

Often, we treat self-control like a hindrance to pure joy and personal happiness when, in actuality, it is the key which unlocks our enslavement to sin. That is why freedom from temptation is found in our ability to tame the tongue and control our desires. It recalibrates our minds to seek holiness in our thoughts and actions rather than yielding to lusts of the flesh which tempt us to sin. When self-control is evident in our lives, we are also less likely to lead others astray when we succumb to temptation. Therefore, when we exhibit self-control daily, our family and friends benefit because our witness and testimony are not hindered by hypocrisy. Instead, they look to us to model Godly behavior.

Nowhere is this more evident than in the taming of the tongue. In the heat of an argument, anger is readily available and willing to burst forth at any moment. When we are being accused or held accountable for our actions, our flesh will always look to defend itself. Like an animal backed into a corner, we will scratch and claw our way out without the slightest regard for the injuries our reckless words cause. In those moments, self-control is our only reprieve from the wrath of anger. The danger is that when we resort to cursing, insults, lies, or blame shifting to protect ourselves, we clearly demonstrate our lack of spiritual maturity to manage our emotions in a healthy and productive manner.

Self-control is not merely a nice-to-have but a need-to-have in our lives. It compensates for our lack of discernment in the moment when we say whatever pops into our minds rather than pausing to think before we speak. It puts us in someone's shoes so we can measure the impact of our words ahead of time before we are forced to accept the consequences of our actions. More importantly, it gets us out of a self-focused mentality because we understand that our actions cast a debris field of destruction. In the end, self-control is the greatest survival tool we have at our disposal, for it keeps us accountable to God. The question is whether we will use it to guard our mouths and control our actions rather than reacting to how our flesh feels in the moment.

Application

1. Why is self-control an essential spiritual discipline to learn?
2. How has self-control guarded you from temptation?
3. In what areas do you struggle exhibiting self-control?
4. How has a lack of self-control caused pain, suffering, and trials in your life?
5. What lessons have you learned observing others who struggle maintaining self-control?
6. How has self-control enabled you to witness the Gospel of Jesus Christ to others more effectively?
7. Why is your attitude toward self-control important to God?
8. What risks do you take by not exhibiting self-control when temptation arises?

Prayer

Lord, thank You for giving me ample opportunity to serve You rather than my flesh. Your provision is always perfect, yet I often fail to utilize the gifts You have given me to choose righteousness over sin. I recognize how my lack of self-control has caused me to wander from the wisdom of Your Word and do things I now regret. I accept the consequences of my actions. I simply ask that You have mercy on me in Your judgment. Temptation is a constant battle for me, but I know I can use self-control to escape any snare of sin the enemy puts before me. Help me continually learn from my foolishness so I may walk in the light of Your truth. Amen.

Day 9 - Fear

"Fear not, for I am with you; be not dismayed, for I am your God;
I will strengthen you, I will help you,
I will uphold you with my righteous right hand."

— Isaiah 41:10 —

Fear has the power of crippling even the strongest man. We can put up a front and act as if we are not scared of anything, but men are just as scared as everyone else. It all comes down to knowing what we are afraid of, what triggers it, and releasing that fear back to God who is the only one powerful enough to do something about it. That does not mean bad things will never happen to us or that God will not allow our faith to be tested in order to push our fears to the surface. It simply means that whatever issues we face, God will not allow us to be tested beyond what He knows we can handle.

One of the biggest challenges in conquering fear is simply asking for help. For whatever reason, men absorb and shoulder the burden of fear rather than releasing it, which only makes the problem worse. What we seem to forget altogether is that Jesus died to free us from the bondage of fear. Death was defeated on the cross of Calvary, yet we still cower in fear of the enemy. Why? Scripture reminds us, **"If God is for us, who can be against us?" (Romans 8:31)**. Therefore, we have nothing to fear because He who spoke creation into existence is sovereign overall and knows what we need even before we do.

Personally, what keeps me up at night is ensuring my wife and daughters are safe and healthy. I constantly pray that the Lord would guard and protect my family. I am not sure why it is so top of mind except that I know my job is to protect my family, and I worry about whether I will always be capable. However, I also know my limitations and that only God can stop bad things from happening when all is said and done. I certainly cannot stop natural disasters from occurring nor predict the motives and intentions of strangers when I take my kids out in public. Honestly, I get extremely nervous when my little girls are not directly next to me whenever we are outside our home. I never want to be in a situation where something horrific happens because I am careless or distracted.

Evil exists all around us, which means I must always be on guard to protect them from harm (as best I can) and ensure their safety. However, I am learning that I cannot allow fear to consume my mind and hinder me from taking risks. It would be easy to assume something bad will happen if we go out in public. Therefore, we should just stay home and avoid all social interaction. However, would I truly be trusting God if fear of man stopped me from living life to the fullest? Moreover, would the Gospel of Jesus Christ reach its full potential if I was afraid to share it out of fear of rejection or persecution?

The sad truth is fear often hinders us from being the hands and feet of Jesus to a lost and broken world. We worry about what others might think, assume, or expect from us, so we hold back and remain quiet. Sometimes, we tend to be so stifled by the fear of every hypothetical outcome possible (which may or may not come to fruition) that we forget about God entirely. We can be so focused on ourselves that He is not even part of the discussion nor the answer to our problems. How can that be?

If God is who He says He is in the pages of Scripture, then we have absolutely nothing to fear because His sovereignty reigns supreme. **"All the nations are as nothing before him, they are accounted by him as less than nothing and emptiness" (Isaiah 40:17)**. God is not immune to our fear and worry but expects that we lay them down at the foot of the cross to finally experience freedom. That is why Jesus died in our place so we did not have to fear judgment. He made a way because we could not. Whom then shall we fear?

For eighteen years, I have worried about all my daughters' safety, yet the Lord is calling me to trust Him time and again. My oldest daughter began college less than three hours away from home and I am no longer there to guard and protect her. I must now put all my trust in God's sovereignty, knowing she belonged to Him long before He gave her to us. Therefore, I have to remind myself daily, whom shall I fear? I am not saying watching my daughter leave the nest has been easy. I have shed many tears over it, but I cannot hold her back from spreading her wings and learning life skills she will never experience if she does not go. Thus, I have learned to let go of my fear and trust the Lord who can protect her in ways I cannot.

It is never easy relinquishing control. We joke about crying out, "Jesus, take the wheel!" when desperation overwhelms our minds and tempts us to lose hope over the uncertain future. However, that is the essence of faith. If we identify as Christ-followers, we cannot act like the world and self-medicate our fears. We serve a holy God, who will never leave or forsake us. Therefore, when we are overcome with anxiety and the enemy tempts us to believe we are all alone, we can rest assured that the Spirit of the living God resides in our hearts and we have nothing to fear. In fact, fear is a liar. So, let us rest in the light of God's absolute truth and take courage.

Application

1. What are you afraid of? What keeps you up at night?
2. What holds you back from talking about your fears?
3. When you feel anxiety beginning to overwhelm your mind, how do you cope in the moment and cast out your fears?
4. How has a fear of persecution hindered you from sharing the Gospel of Jesus Christ?
5. What regrets do you have allowing fear to hold you back from living life to the fullest?
6. What difference does it make knowing God is sovereign?
7. What fear-based lies are tormenting your mind?
8. How can you display a reverent fear of God more often?

Prayer

Lord, Your provision is perfect and Your blessings are abundant. Why then do I doubt that You will help me overcome my fears? I cannot explain why I succumb to fear so often or why I worry about things beyond my control. My perspective is more glass-half-empty than glass-half-full. I tend to focus my attention on what is wrong. All I know is that fear has waged war on my psyche for far too long and I am tired of being tormented by the enemy. Please give me courage to face my fears and reject Satan's lies. Help me trust that You always know what is best for me. You are sovereign and I need to stop believing that I am all alone in my trials and suffering. Help me see Your Spirit moving all around me for my good. Amen.

Day 10 – Courage

"Have I not commanded you? Be strong and courageous. Do not be frightened, and do not be dismayed, for the Lord your God is with you wherever you go."

— Joshua 1:9 —

It seems so easy to step outside our homes and engage this world with unwavering courage that nothing can stop us. When we read about the life of Joshua, it is easy to see that trusting God is the right decision because we read about what happened from hindsight perspective. In the moment, trusting that God would enable Israel's army to defeat the giants before them was difficult. On paper, Israel was at a huge disadvantage, yet Joshua knew the Lord's army could not be defeated. From his vantage point, victory was guaranteed!

Joshua was strong in faith because he did not forget the incredible miracles God performed in the wilderness. He had seen the Lord move supernaturally and his faith was emboldened because of it. When spies were sent out to survey the promised land, only Joshua and Caleb responded by faith that God would honor His Word despite the obstacles before them which seemed insurmountable. Their faith in the Lord inspired courage, and we are wise to recognize how deep our roots of faith run if we expect God to do what only He can do when we ask for His help in prayer.

I stand amazed by the brave men and women who serve in positions which require them to run into a fire rather than away from it. I have never served in the military nor worked as a police officer or fireman, but I have utmost respect for those who do and the enormous price they pay for pushing their personal comforts aside to help those in need. I have friends who suffer from post-traumatic stress disorder and it breaks my heart to hear their stories of tragedy on the front lines. What they have seen and experienced is indescribable to those of us who have never walked a mile in their shoes. As a result, they deserve our support and respect. For when we are in an emergency, all we care about is their ability to help us.

Courage takes on many forms that we often fail to see the power of simply trusting God when the mountains seem as if they cannot be moved. Prospective parents who sit in a doctor's office and are told the likelihood of their child being born with a chronic disability is one example. Culture would say the answer to their problem is clear: abort the child and end the pregnancy, because who wants to spend the rest of their lives caring for a special needs child? However, courage enables us to step into the fire and face adversity with the understanding that no matter what happens, we will accept the hand we are dealt and glorify God regardless.

There is incredible power when we trust the Lord and act with courage despite adversity. For example, it takes courage to forgive those who have hurt us or speak truth in the lives of people caught in the chains of addiction. Courage empowers us to speak boldly for righteousness when others are silent or stand for the unborn who have no voice to protect themselves. There are countless examples of what courage looks like to inspire our behavior. We just need to open our eyes and learn from those who have trusted God's sovereignty so we can also rely on His strength rather than our own.

I am inspired by my wife's courage. After having three daughters, we were blessed years ago with another pregnancy which ended in miscarriage at 11-weeks. At that point, though we had lost the baby,

Amber still needed a D&C procedure which could have been medically administered or done naturally. She decided to avoid the hospital and go home trusting that God would protect her. Thankfully, her body naturally purged what it needed, but we did not expect how much blood she would lose in the process. Unfortunately, she had to immediately be rushed to the hospital to save her life after passing out on our bathroom floor due to extreme blood loss.

That experience was traumatic for our family. Words cannot begin to describe the pain a mother experiences losing a child to miscarriage. A father can attempt to relate, but it is just not the same. However, Amber would not be shaken. In her mind, **"The LORD gave, and the LORD has taken away; blessed be the name of the LORD" (Job 1:21).** She knew God was still sovereign and His purpose for what had happened would be revealed in due time. Therefore, she clung to her faith in Jesus and would not allow the enemy to steal her joy. In the end, God did bless us with a fourth daughter soon after, but I am forever reminded of Amber's courage to trust the Lord despite the pain and anguish she endured.

Courage is not limited to displays of great power or strength. It is often exhibited in the simple acts of life which seem insignificant. However, the greater question is whether our faith inspires courage to obey the Lord's will for our lives. For without Jesus Christ, courage is devoid of value, meaning, and purpose. Granted, we can strongarm our way through life and achieve some semblance of success by determination and the sweat of our brow. However, we will never grow to our full potential spiritually without the Lord providing the courage we need to face our trials and tribulations with joy and confidence.

Application

1. How would you define courage? What does it look like?
2. Who inspires courage in you based on their Christ-like example? Why?
3. Give an example of a time where you acted courageously. What did you learn from that experience?
4. How can you walk by faith courageously?
5. Why are you reluctant at times to obey the Lord's calling and courageously obey His will?
6. Why is forgiveness such a powerful act of courage? How have you forgiven others which you never thought possible?
7. If the Spirit of God lives in you, why do you submit to fear rather than trust the Lord with unwavering confidence?

Prayer

Lord, You are my provider and protector, the rock in whom I trust completely. Why then do I cower in fear rather than stand boldly and courageously? The more I reflect, the more Your Spirit convicts my soul that courage is an act of faith which I am lacking and must remedy. I am humbled by Your grace which You pour out so lavishly. Help me to never take that priceless gift for granted but to trust Your sovereignty. I cannot predict the future but I do not need to, because You know the beginning and the end of my trials. Please continue to inspire me through the courage I see in others according to their example of unwavering faith in You. Amen.

Day 11 - Deception

"Do not be deceived: God is not mocked, for whatever one sows, that will he also reap. For the one who sows to his own flesh will from the flesh reap corruption, but the one who sows to the Spirit will from the Spirit reap eternal life."

— *Galatians 6:7-8* —

How can a man maintain Godly character if his words and actions are not genuine? How can we have a clear conscience if we mislead others to believe we are the same publicly as privately when clearly we are not? Deception is one of the most slippery slopes we navigate in our lives. It is not a blatant sin we intentionally focus our attention on remedying because it can appear minor or insignificant in the grand scheme of things. However, the more we allow deception to simmer along the battleground of our minds, the greater opportunity it has to permeate every aspect of our thoughts and behavior like a deadly virus.

We have all told little white lies to avoid owning our sins and the consequences of our actions. How then do we stop? The biggest challenge with deception is how easily it can begin. Bending the truth seems irrelevant in the moment, which is why we run with it rather than correcting our behavior. Over time, what once felt guilty does not shake us anymore. We become numb, indifferent, and desensitized to moral truth, so much that we cannot distinguish right from wrong. It is a precarious situation we find ourselves in when conviction is absent from our lives. It should signal how far from grace we have truly fallen and how much we need help getting back up to draw unto Christ.

Regrettably, I cannot begin to count the number of lies I told Amber throughout the early years of our marriage about my struggle with lust. She knew my libido was high, but she assumed it was because all men are wired that way. It was not until we were married that she caught me looking at pornography. At that moment, she realized I had a much bigger problem than simply craving sex all the time like most guys. I was lost spiritually. My mind had become numb to the truth of Scripture and I felt little remorse in my heart to overcome my addiction and honor my marriage vows. I was a religious hypocrite who could not distinguish right from wrong.

It is humbling to admit how deceptive I once was. I regret not confessing my sins to Amber long before we walked down the aisle. At a minimum, she deserved to know the truth of my addiction to discern whether she still wanted to marry me. She also needed to know whether I was willing to seek Biblical counseling to change my ways before we committed our lives to one another. However, she was forced to deal with the reality of my sins after the fact and endure intense spiritual warfare which ensued. Insecurities and self-doubt plagued her mind for years. They still haunt her to this day, even though she was innocent. The problem was my unwillingness to change which drug her into the destructive path of my sins.

What we rarely recognize about deception is the impact it has on those we love. Collateral damage is rampant when we choose to cover our tracks and hide our guilty pleasures. The problem is when we crawl out from the shadows and into the light, a wake of destruction will surely follow and force us to reconcile the reality of what we have done. When we sin, there are innocent bystanders who get caught in the crossfire and absorb the trauma of our foolish decisions. We may not want to accept that others are directly impacted by our sins, but who are we fooling if we believe sin exists in a vacuum, completely separate from the rest of our lives?

The apostle Paul's warning in Galatians 6:7-8 has proven true time and again for countless generations. Undoubtedly, we reap what we sow. We may not experience the consequences of our actions today, but rest assured, we will in the future if we do not stop our deception, turn toward the light of Christ, and repent of our sins. Jesus said, **"I tell you, on the day of judgment people will give account for every careless word they speak, for by your words you will be justified, and by your words you will be condemned" (Matthew 12:36–37)**. Therefore, we are wise to recognize the power of our words when we mislead others to believe we are holy and righteous. God will not be mocked nor will He turn a blind eye toward our sins. Therefore, we will give account on judgment day for our thoughts and actions, whether we like it or not, which should terrify us mightily.

A man of Godly character cannot allow deception to take root in his heart, but that is often easier said than done. Opportunity will arise to test how committed we are to live in the light of God's Word rather than the dark shadows of self-protection. Satan knows if he can deceive us into questioning the validity of God's commands, we will take hold of the forbidden fruit and taste it without considering how our foolish decisions impact others. Therefore, if we desire to reap the blessings of righteousness in our lives, we must first sow seeds of honesty and confess our sins to one another. God has graciously given us free will to choose which path we will take in life, but we must choose wisely or inevitably suffer the immense consequences of our deception entirely.

Application

1. How easy is it for you tell a lie? Why is that?
2. Why are lying lips an abomination to the Lord?
3. If the smallest, white lie can sentence you to hell for eternity, why would you allow deception to take root in your heart?
4. What level of conviction do you experience when you lie or mislead others? How so?
5. What consequences of actions have you faced because you manipulated the truth?
6. What motivation do you have to inspire lasting change in your heart?
7. How can you seek wise counsel to hold you accountable from lying and deception?

Prayer

Lord, I have sinned against You first and foremost. Please forgive me for how prone I have become to misleading and lying to others. I own my sins and the wake of destruction I have caused. I am not the righteous man I claim to be, but I know I can change by the power of Your Spirit living in me. Convict me of my sins, Lord. Reveal the evil and wickedness I have allowed to reign supreme in my heart. Truly, I am self-deceived by temptation and need the light of Your Word to shine in the darkest shadows of my soul. I humble myself before You and pray that You completely break me of my sins. Help me live for righteousness and die to deceptive tendencies all the days of my life. Amen.

Day 12 - Honesty

"Let what you say be simply 'Yes' or 'No'; anything more than this comes from evil."

— Matthew 5:37 —

Have you ever heard the phrase, "Honesty is the best policy?" Well, it is if we are being honest! The difficulty we face when it comes to telling the truth is to what degree should we be honest. For example, if a wife puts on a dress which makes her look bigger than she truly is, should her husband honestly respond, "Yes, honey, that dress makes you look fat!" or tell her what she wants to hear instead? Which is the lesser of two evils? At some point, most guys find themselves in no-win situations where honesty will only make things worse and dishonesty will produce the same result. How then should we respond as Godly men?

The key is learning how to speak truth in love so we are never avoiding honesty or bending the truth but measuring our words. We must build others up rather than tearing them down. Keep in mind, that does not mean we resort to lying to spare someone's feelings, but we seek to edify and encourage in every situation. Certainly, it takes an incredible amount of practice to make perfect, but God expects us to hold honesty in high regard as one of the most critical aspects of our personal character. We cannot be misleading or deceitful in any situation and expect others to respect our integrity. For if we expect to be given the benefit of the doubt, we must accept honesty entirely.

In many ways, honesty has been an integral part of the sales success over my career. I hold firm to Matthew 5:37 and share my thoughts and opinions freely with those who ask. However, I have learned to season my words because I often lean too heavily on blunt honesty rather than truth spoken in love. Sometimes, my bluntness has been problematic. Other times, it has been exactly what the doctor ordered. Regardless, I have learned to implement accountability by how I communicate and conduct myself within my company and with customers as well.

For instance, if an important email must be sent, I have my manager proofread what I have written to soften the edges so that the message is not lost in translation by my blunt demeanor. I am certainly not afraid of speaking up and calling a spade a spade when others remain silent, but I am also careful to not cause division by speaking truth out of frustration. It has been a journey, but I am far better than I used to be sharing my opinion in a collaborative manner which is solution-based and not divisive. In the end, I have earned the respect of my colleagues and customers over the years because I have held a high standard of honesty and moral character.

Because deception is such a slippery slope and morphs over time, we must take truthfulness very seriously. It begins with applying a non-negotiable, zero-tolerance standard in our homes which conveys that lying will not be tolerated in any way, especially with our children. When deceit begins to shape the character of those we love, we should address the problem rather than brush it under the rug. Those who have no problems lying or being deceptive will only suffer greater consequences in the future, which may be too late to rectify based on the severity of their addictive behavior. Therefore, we are wise to address things earlier rather than later and make changes now before they make matters worse.

However, we must stop and gauge whether the destructive pattern of dishonesty we see in others mirrors our own reflection. We can point the finger and blame cultural influence all we want for our decisions, but we should always model the behavior we expect from others. That is why Jesus said, **"How can you say to your brother, 'Let me take the speck out of your eye,' when there is the log in your own eye? You hypocrite, first take the log out of your own eye, and then you will see clearly to take the speck out of your brother's eye" (Matthew 7:4–5)**. Failure to examine our hearts, first and foremost, only breeds hypocrisy and a lack of respect from others.

Deception in this world will only change if we are willing to swallow our pride and accept personal responsibility for being part of the problem rather than the solution. That is a difficult pill to swallow but necessary to put an end to lying and deceit. Therefore, if we want to make a huge difference in this world, we must humble ourselves and examine where we have been the source of deception or simply allowed it to fester. Only then will we remedy the patterns of dishonesty which plague our hearts and create relational bitterness and dissension. Honesty is never easy because it is terribly convicting, but it is necessary to build up the kingdom of heaven.

In the end, integrity is dependent upon speaking truth in love to others and completely owning our failures. Granted, not everyone will appreciate the honesty we share, but they will likely respect us more for being willing to speak truth rather than remaining silent or indifferent. Therefore, we must boldly share the truth of the Gospel so that others come to faith in Christ and receive salvation. For hell is real, and the world needs to know what awaits them if they do not repent of their sins and accept Jesus Christ as Lord and Savior. Tomorrow is not guaranteed which means we must act now.

Application

1. How is honesty an integral part of preserving integrity?
2. Which areas of your life are you more honest vs. dishonest?
3. Why is it critical to be brutally honest with yourself before being honest with others?
4. What are the dangers associated with truth spoken harshly?
5. How can you be more loving with the honesty you share?
6. When are you prone to bend the truth or tell a lie?
7. Why did Jesus say, **"Let what you say be simply 'Yes' or 'No?'"** What was the point of His teaching?
8. How can you implement accountability with honesty to ensure what you communicate is not lost in translation?

Prayer

Lord, I confess that I struggle being honest across all areas of my life. I tend to pick and choose when and where I am genuine and with whom I am honest, which makes no sense. I recognize the foolishness in my behavior and pray that You expose selfish areas of my character which need pruning. I have no reason to self-protect by bending the truth and telling lies. All I know is that I need Your strength to start living for holiness rather than wasting my time covering my tracks and avoiding the consequences of my actions. I want to be a man of integrity across all areas of my life. Therefore, honesty must become a hill I am willing to die on. Otherwise, Satan will lead me astray once again and away from Your holy presence. Help me to embrace honesty, Lord, no matter the cost. Amen.

Day 13 - Manipulation

"Beware of false prophets, who come to you in sheep's clothing but inwardly are ravenous wolves."

— Matthew 7:15 —

What man is willing to look at himself in the mirror and admit he is guilty of manipulation? Honesty of that magnitude feels harsh, especially if we are unwilling to dive into the deep waters of self-examination and confess guilt in this particular area. Truly, manipulation is the exit strategy or accessible escape route when we sin against God and others. Its sole purpose is to cover our tracks and avoid consequences directly related to our sins. Any man unwilling to admit he is a manipulator when the mask of his false reputation is exposed is spiritually blind to his own blindness, because he cannot perceive the truth from a lie. Nonetheless, he walks around believing he can, much to his destruction!

Manipulation is one of those sins which is present before and after we choose to disobey God's Word. When we are consumed with the idols of our affection, a strategy is put into place to get us from point 'A' to point 'B.' Manipulation is the mode of transportation which allows us to crossover from light to darkness so we can access the pleasures of this world more easily. It is not the object of our affection but the required tool to make it happen. It is also what we use to ensure no one discovers our guilty pleasures so we can access them anytime we want. In other words, manipulation is the bridge to fantasy island and the pleasures of this world.

Do not be mistaken. Being a manipulator does not mean we are naïve in the slightest. Rather, we are fully aware of what we are doing when we orchestrate our way toward satisfying the flesh and covering up our sins. Just as sin is a volitional choice we make to disobey God's truth and chase after false idols, manipulation is a conscious decision to strategically navigate the consequences of sin and accountability. It specializes in lying and deception by creating smokescreens to escape personal responsibility, ownership of sins, and genuine repentance. Truly, manipulation may be our most serious indicator of bondage and enslavement to sin than anything else in our lives.

I spent two decades of my life addicted to pornography. Though I knew it was wrong, I could not break the cycle of fantasizing about whether the grass was greener on the other side. That is the problem with sin, though. It is never satisfied but only craves more. Inevitably, I found myself transitioning from magazines to videos and the internet to satisfy my desire for inspiration so that I could gratify myself. My debased mind craved images to lust over to fuel my fantasies, and I was committed to ensure my carnal desires were satisfied, however and whenever I pleased.

Unfortunately, even after Amber discovered my addiction and boundaries were placed into my life, I still felt drawn to sin like a moth to a flame. Sadly, I had not hit rock bottom. Determined to repair the bridge to fantasy island, I began manipulating my story that I was a changed man who would never cross the line and have an affair. However, I was just a hypocrite who chose to keep sin's embers burning rather than extinguish the fires of lust. I wish I could say I chose the right path, but I failed. Only when my day of reckoning came to fruition and Amber was tempted to divorce me did I finally die to sin and begin the process of restoration.

Day 13 - Manipulation

When we sober up and recognize our sin as spiritual death, we come face-to-face with the harsh reality of who we have become apart from Christ. That is why the forbidden fruit Adam and Eve ate was from the tree of knowledge of good and evil. When they bit down and swallowed its sweet nectar, their eyes were opened and the reality of their sin came to light. Their hearts were overwhelmed with guilt, shame, and regret, and that is exactly what happens to us when our moment of clarity comes to fruition. We recognize how easily we have been deceived and disobeyed the Lord.

The grass is actually not greener on the other side. It is simply greener where we water it, for better or worse. Thus, if we are manipulating conditions to satisfy our sinful desires, we will reap what we sow tenfold. However, if we straighten up and fly right, we will guard our minds from believing Satan's lies that greater pleasures exist outside the boundaries of God's sovereign provision. Indeed, too much of a good thing can be detrimental if manipulated for selfish pleasure. Therefore, we must be wise as serpents (Matt. 10:16) to ensure we are not baited into feeling discontent about God's provision.

In my case, God's greatest gift (outside of salvation) is my wife. However, I was once discontent in my marriage because my desire was only to please myself instead of selflessly loving and serving her. I failed to recognize what a blessing she is until God broke my selfish pride and exposed my hypocrisy. I have since learned that lust was not my ultimate problem. It was simply the fruit of my sin. The real cancer, love of self, lurked well beneath the surface of my heart. Therefore, it was not until I died to love of self and God exposed my manipulation that change began to take root in my heart. Only then was our broken marriage reconciled, restored, and redeemed by God's grace.

Application

1. How would you define manipulation? What makes it evil?
2. What do you ultimately risk if you manipulate others?
3. Have you ever considered yourself a master manipulator? Why or why not?
4. How has God broken your pride and revealed that the grass is not greener on the other side?
5. What scars do you bear from manipulating others to believe you were a Godly man when clearly you were not?
6. What guilt, shame, and regret do you bear that is linked to the manipulation you used to hide your sins and cover your tracks?
7. What personal boundaries must you implement to guard against manipulating others for selfish gain?

Prayer

Lord, I have never considered myself a master manipulator, but Your Spirit has convicted me that I have played the hearts and minds of others like puppets to hide my sins from their knowledge. I am ashamed of my wickedness and being consumed by sin. Help me become humble, broken, and repentant. Like David, I ask that You create in me a clean heart. Renew a right spirit within me which honors Your Word and glorifies Your presence. I am saved by grace because of Your unending love, Lord. I do not deserve Your mercy but I sincerely thank You for loving me enough to expose my sins and break my pride. Help me to never again manipulate others into believing I am more righteous than I truly am. Amen.

Day 14 - Trust

> *"When I am afraid, I put my trust in you. In God, whose word I praise, in God I trust; I shall not be afraid. What can flesh do to me?"*
>
> — Psalm 56:3-4 —

What do we do when we have broken trust with our loved ones? Walk away or rebuild? The reality is that when we have morally failed, we must confess and repent to God and those we have sinned against so that they have full opportunity to forgive us. However, the buck stops there! Though we may be forgiven, rebuilding trust is a completely different issue to overcome. There is no timetable when others will trust us again. It is a slow and methodical process, contingent upon consistency of behavioral changes which affirm our remorse is real and we understand the damages we have caused.

Honestly, our biggest complaint is about forgetting rather than forgiving. Deep within our hearts, we hope and pray others will somehow experience spiritual amnesia and forget about our sins altogether. From our perspective, it is easy to identify with King David's honest admission, **"For I know my transgressions, and my sin is ever before me" (Psalm 51:3).** If we have sinned grievously against those we see practically every day, the memory of our consequences is constant. We cannot escape them no matter how hard we try. However, the same logic holds true for our victims as they continue to forgive us daily for the pain and suffering our sins have caused them.

That is why we often struggle to move on from the past because we cannot escape the consequences of our sins nor the memories of who we once were apart from Christ. If something triggers others to remember details from our confession, wounds can easily be ripped open again and painful memories can come flooding back just like it was yesterday. That is why trust is so difficult to regain and rebuild. It seems relatively easy, but reality is completely different when our present sins mirror those of the past. Moreover, our enemy is always seeking ways to keep our former sins current so that we never fully escape the memory of their destructive wake.

Without question, I completely obliterated any semblance of trust I had with Amber when I sat her down and confessed my affair. However, I was determined to live in the light of truth, so I answered every question she had about my past to prove I was broken and repentant. In retrospect, she regrets that decision because memories now haunt her mentally and spiritually. However, to begin the process of reconciliation, I had to embrace honesty and humble myself like never before by being truthful about whatever details she wanted to know.

What we have experienced over time has been spiritual warfare which has tested the depth and breadth of our marriage and Amber's faith. Though my confession plagued her mind, she never felt the love of Christ so intimately than when the truth of my sins came to light. She understood the betrayal Jesus felt and found comfort in Scripture which encouraged her to forgive. It took over a decade before she fully trusted me again, but that did not matter. I was willing to wait forever if it meant having a second chance to honor my marriage vows and forsake all others till death do us part.

Keep in mind, there is no blueprint for how long it takes to rebuild trust with those we have sinned against. Every situation is different and every individual unique. Some may trust again quickly; others may take a long while. Still others will refuse to trust and walk away bitter and angry. The key is not putting expectations on time but learning to rely on God's sovereignty instead. For when the time comes, God will reveal whether the changes we have made are credible and trustworthy. Therefore, we do not have to speak up and remind others how much we believe we have changed. Our actions will speak for themselves and the Lord will testify on our behalf if we are truly repentant.

Wounds can run deep, though. Depending on the severity of our sins, complete trust may never again come to fruition. However, some semblance of trust is better than none at all to heal open wounds. If we are not content with that reality, then we must reevaluate whether our remorse is truly genuine. Truly, we revoked our rights to a fair trial the minute we spat in the face of God and pulled our loved ones through the mud due to our sins. Therefore, the last thing we should ever do is complain about how long it takes for them to forgive and forget. If we are indeed repentant, receiving forgiveness is blessing enough to spend the rest of our lives in full gratitude to Christ for cleansing our sins.

I have thought long and hard about Amber's trust and what a gift it is to me. Before my confession, I took it for granted. Now, I understand its infinite value and never again want to lose it. In theory, trust based on benefit of the doubt is appreciated. However, because I broke her heart, being given a second chance to reconcile our marriage is indescribable. I know I do not deserve her grace and mercy, but I am incredibly thankful for it because I now understand why trust is a priceless gift. Therefore, I embrace it with humility, gratitude, and respect because I know how it feels to lose it, and I do not want to risk failing as a Godly husband and father ever again.

Application

1. Why is trust a precious gift you have freely been given?
2. What are the risks of abusing someone's faith and trust?
3. Why do you trust God? How has He clearly made Himself known to you?
4. Give an example of how someone has broken your trust. How easy or difficult was it for you to forgive vs. forget?
5. Why is it wise to avoid placing expectations when others should move on from the memories of your sinful past?
6. How have you rebuilt trust with those you have grievously sinned against? What made the difference between success and failure?
7. Who are you unwilling to trust? Why can you not forgive and forget?

Prayer

Lord, You have made Yourself known to me in so many ways. I am overwhelmed by the grace and mercy You have shown me despite my failures. Thank You for being the rock whom I trust unconditionally. Many friends and family members have come and gone, but You have been ever faithful. Help me reflect the same character quality to my family so they know they can always trust and depend on me. Conform me to the image of Christ in all I say and do so my words are trustworthy and always spoken in love. I may not be a perfect man, but I desire to be transformed by the power of Your Word in my heart and mind. Amen.

Day 15 – Laziness

"I passed by the field of a sluggard, by the vineyard of a man lacking sense, and behold, it was all overgrown with thorns; the ground was covered with nettles, and its stone wall was broken down. Then I saw and considered it; I looked and received instruction. A little sleep, a little slumber, a little folding of the hands to rest, and poverty will come upon you like a robber, and want like an armed man."

— *Proverbs 24:30-34* —

Today's Scripture passage is a powerful warning on the dangers of laziness. It begs the question whether we resemble the man who passed by or the one who owned the vineyard. If the former, we likely realize the power of self-recognition and personal discipline to achieve our goals. If the latter, chances are we are spiritually blind to our own blindness and incapable of putting in the blood, sweat, and tears to change our lazy habits and slothful tendencies.

Work is not a result of the Fall. From the beginning, Adam was tasked to work in the Garden of Eden because idleness was never part of God's original plan. We were made to be creative and use our gifts for productive purposes, yet we often look for ways to avoid working altogether rather than grinding away to yield a good harvest for our labor. The greater danger of laziness is missing out on opportunities to learn and stretch our faith, for spiritual growth will never occur in our hearts if we are not working diligently to live out the Gospel of Jesus Christ daily.

God's Word is full of wisdom. However, we will miss all the Lord has in store for us if we are unwilling to be molded by the power of the Holy Spirit as we apply what Scripture teaches. True spiritual growth comes when we transition from laziness to active participation. Refusing to work is simply disobedience to God's Word. No man can complain about receiving an empty harvest if he has not worked to till the soil, plant the seed, and water the roots. God will provide light to make the seed grow, but we must take the first step to work diligently to prepare the soil.

For many years, I was a lazy Christian. My faith was shallow and stagnant. I went to church every Sunday and tried to be a good person, but I was simply going through the motions. I wore my faith on my sleeve and did what I thought Christians were supposed to do, even though it felt like I was stuck in neutral. I could not understand why I felt so empty until I realized something profound which inevitably changed my life forever. Namely, I was held captive by the restrictions of organized religion when what I really needed was a personal relationship with Jesus Christ and fresh perspective on what God's Word teaches.

In the Catholic church where I grew up, taking personal responsibility for studying the Bible was never preached. I was spoon-fed a weekly dose of Scripture readings till the next Sunday rolled around. As a result, my personal growth was extremely shallow and lazy. I went through the motions like a wandering sheep and found myself lost in the pasture of the church which made no sense to me. It was not until I attended a different denomination years later, which challenged me to take responsibility for my faith, that I began to see changes in my character and how God called me to live. I had to die to religion and personally engage my faith in a relationship with Jesus to grow spiritually.

The problem is we often do not see how distracted we have become until it is too late. Simply consider the amount of time men devote to sports or videogaming as prime examples of how easily we ignore the needs of others when we are hopelessly addicted to entertainment and selfish pleasure. Laziness is not necessarily something dependent on staying home and lying on the couch. It can be just as dangerous when we are so busy pleasing our flesh that we ignore the greater responsibilities of our lives to which we are held accountable.

For instance, I was once lazy reading devotions with my girls before bed. I knew they were important. But when I got to the end of the day exhausted and worn out, I just wanted to tuck the kids in bed and enjoy some down time. However, Amber pointed out my sin, held me spiritually accountable, and challenged me to stop making excuses. She reminded me that it did not matter that my father never read devotions to me growing up. I was the spiritual leader of our home and needed to shepherd our girls better. It was a tough pill to swallow but one I desperately needed to hear.

Laziness is often very discreet. It does not draw attention to itself or come across as blatantly obvious. Instead, it is a bare minimum character flaw which builds over time. We do not wake up one morning and decide to be a lazy sloth. Rather, it is a degradation process which morphs over time. Before we know it, months and years have passed since we stepped up to the plate and disciplined ourselves to be the spiritual leaders God expects. Perhaps that is why God chose a simple ant to teach us the wisdom of avoiding laziness and working hard instead! **"Go to the ant, O sluggard; consider her ways, and be wise" (Proverbs 6:6).**

Application

1. Why is laziness so easy to identify but difficult to change?
2. Would you consider yourself a lazy man? Why or why not?
3. How does laziness typically manifest itself in your life? Why is it important to recognize where you are lazy?
4. Who suffers most when you are lazy and indifferent about spiritual disciplines?
5. Why does God have so much to say about laziness?
6. What is one area of laziness you can focus your attention on fixing? What difference would it make?
7. What is one lazy thing you do to ignore accountability?
8. Why are you so hardhearted about changing your behavior?

Prayer

Lord, I often look at work as a begrudging chore I have to do rather than something I get to do. I always thought having to work to make ends meet was a curse from Adam. Now I recognize how You mold and shape my character when I step forward in faith and work hard to make positive changes happen. Please open my eyes to areas where I am spiritually blind to the negative impact my laziness causes. Help me be a more Godly leader—one who is diligent and committed to humbling himself daily. I know I need to do better in this area. Break me of my pride, Lord, and encourage me to own my sin of laziness. I no longer want to be a poor example of Godly character in my home, but rather one who works hard to live for righteousness. Amen.

Day 16 – Purpose

"For I know the plans I have for you, declares the Lord, plans for welfare and not for evil, to give you a future and a hope."

— Jeremiah 29:11 —

"What is my purpose in life?" There is not a man alive (past or present) who has not thought about that question at some point or filtered it through his past, present, and future in the hope of finding answers. A man without divine purpose is like a ship without a rudder. He will wander aimlessly, blown to and fro by the wind with no tool to guide his path. Without a goal in mind, we can get lost in worldly pleasures and fall victim to a myriad of sinful temptations. Therefore, we have a choice to make. Live life to the fullest as if tomorrow were our last, or plan wisely for the future and surrender to God's authority?

The problem with never looking past tomorrow is how narrow-minded it is toward our role of provision. We may live for a hundred years for all we know, so living without direction and devoid of purpose is foolish. Life demands we plan for the future because our role as husbands and fathers is to provide and protect our families. We can certainly live with a focus squarely on today, but we must plan wisely for what tomorrow may bring. God has a unique purpose and plan for each of our lives, but that requires we stop living for selfish pleasure and seek a higher calling which testifies to our faith in Christ.

I never dreamt I would work in corporate sales. As a teenager, I actively performed in music and theatre, but I was smart enough to realize that neither of those professions were lucrative. All I knew was that I wanted to get out of the crime-prevalent city where I grew up. So, I went off to college with little purpose or direction outside of getting a bachelor's degree in something and never returning home. In retrospect, I wish I would have prayerfully considered God's Word with my education and chose to discern His will for my life. Yet despite my naïve methodology, I chose to pursue a business degree which led me to the company I work for today.

Unfortunately, God was never a part of my decision-making process where I decided to work. It all came down to who provided the best compensation package. I was committed to climb the corporate ladder and make a name for myself. I also wanted to prove that a young man who paid his way through college could reach the mountaintop. My determination made me too scared to fail, but my end goal lacked divine purpose. I was simply living for the world and chasing after financial status. It was not until I started reading my Bible that I realized how foolish I had become and how much I needed God to wreck my self-image so I could live for His glory instead.

It seems so easy to proclaim publicly that we will reject the world and live for Jesus, but saying and doing are completely different. When we accept Jesus as Lord and Savior, we tend to cling to His saving grace but struggle relinquishing control back to Him. Submitting to the lordship of Christ means we must give up everything we hold dear and commit our lives—all that we have and all who we are—for His glory. That is no easy task because aligning our will with God's sovereignty requires that we surrender our pride and relinquish control to the Holy Spirit who guides us.

For instance, can we acknowledge that all we have belongs to God? Are we willing to abandon our personal hobbies and spend time ministering to our families instead? Does obedience compel us to say, "Yes, Lord!" when the Spirit prompts us to serve those less fortunate and preach the Gospel to strangers? Truly, there are many ways to gauge our spiritual temperature and determine whether we have clear direction in life. However, we often find ourselves struggling to discover our divine purpose when laziness interferes with what God wants to do in and through us for His glory.

Case in point, I am an author who is passionate about teaching men, from a Scriptural lens, how to develop Godly character. However, sometimes I wonder why I have spent over half my life working in sales. Nevertheless, life has taught me that corporate America is as much a mission field as countries around the world where Christianity is persecuted. I can be a missionary right where God has placed me. I just need to shift my perspective and open my eyes to see that the fields are white for harvest (John 4:35). I can be a minister of the Gospel in the workforce by how I conduct myself daily with honesty and integrity, which has opened up doors to boldly share my faith in Christ with others as well.

Just because we may not be pastors or missionaries does not mean God cannot use us for His glory. Quite the contrary! God's Word is full of examples of ordinary people being used to do extraordinary things. He has always used broken vessels to advance His kingdom throughout the world and we are part of His plan of salvation. In the end, we must relinquish control of our lives to God and allow Him to use us as He sees fit. Only then will we profit more than we could ever ask for or imagine, because we finally realize that our divine purpose is all about living for the glory of Jesus Christ and not our own.

Application

1. Do you know the plans God has for you? Why or why not?
2. What role does God's sovereignty play in your life?
3. Why is it so important to remember your eternal purpose? What benefit does it serve?
4. How have you floundered spiritually searching for value and significance in all the wrong places?
5. What difference does it make knowing you go no place by accident because God has a plan and purpose for your life?
6. What is something the Spirit prompted you to do that you refused? What did you learn from that experience?
7. What has been your purpose in life thus far? Why?

Prayer

Lord, You know the plans You have for me, but sometimes I doubt whether I truly believe You do. Life seems to test my patience when things do not turn out the way I think they should, which makes me doubt whether I am doing what You ask me to do. There is a lot of noise in my head and I just want to escape from the pressure I feel to discover my purpose. I am learning, though, that while my life's purpose is to glorify You, my daily purpose is to trust the Holy Spirit and obey Your Word. I keep expecting to be used in some mighty way, but that is not always how You work. I see now that You are simply telling me to wait on Your timing and provision, so that is what I will determine my heart and mind to do from this day forward. Amen.

Day 17 - Complaining

> *"Do all things without grumbling or disputing, that you may be blameless and innocent, children of God without blemish in the midst of a crooked and twisted generation, among whom you shine as lights in the world."*
>
> — *Philippians 2:14-15* —

One of the greatest challenges in life is learning how to tame the tongue and resist complaining. When life does not turn out the way we think it should, it is relatively easy to let our thoughts be known and dwell upon negativity. The problem with complaining is it entrenches us deeper into despair and permeates those around us. Like cancer, it spreads from our hearts and minds to theirs, infecting us with a glass-half-empty attitude which solves nothing. Negative attitudes merely breed discontentment and make matters worse, because they are consumed with problems rather than solutions.

Complaining is also heavily influenced by personal opinions which may not be valid. Oftentimes, we make assumptions and treat them as credible facts when the exact opposite may be true. Our limited perception might not be the most trusted piece of information we should be basing our opinion upon. Therefore, it is critical we sift truth from lies before we jump to conclusions and start complaining about what we think we know. That is how gossip starts and we must guard our minds from making snap judgments and swift decisions based on personal assumptions rather than absolute truth.

Sometimes, we simply do not have all the information we need. It may not be that our perception is entirely off but more that our knowledge is severely limited. We are not all-knowing and omniscient like God. We cannot predict the future (though we act as if we can) no matter how hard we try. We simply do not know what others are going through either, because we have not walked a mile in their shoes. In other words, we may not be privy to information which could bring understanding to our attention and help us avoid reacting with poor attitudes and making our opinions known.

Case in point, consider a time when you ate at a restaurant and received poor service. The server's attitude was negative, your drinks were rarely refilled, and the order came out cold and all wrong. In that instance, it would be easy to voice your frustration and complain to the manager. However, what if that server received a serious health diagnosis earlier that day? What if her car broke down on the way to work? What if she was the victim of verbal or physical abuse at home? They are a million scenarios we could hypothesize to explain why the service we received was poor. However, does that even matter?

What if we were aware of the reasons why our service was poor? Would we still complain or be more understanding and content with the service we received, all things considered? The danger with complaining is that it is 100% self-focused. No one else matters when all is said and done, yet that is not how Jesus calls us to live. He expects us to put the needs of others before our own—to still leave a generous tip when we receive the worst service possible rather than the best. He calls us to put off complaining by giving thanks for what we have, instead of what we lack. In other words, He calls us to be content.

Day 17 - Complaining

I will be the first to admit, I struggle with complaining. It is easy for me to pick apart foolishness I see, and nowhere is this more relevant than in my day-to-day job in corporate America. When production is delayed, supply chain has bottlenecks, or my customer does not execute a program like we had planned, I can easily default to frustration and complaining. Rather than helping find a solution, I allow my attitude to go below the line and point the finger, which truly solves nothing. Moreover, I tend to make my opinions known publicly, which does not help the situation but only makes things worse.

The challenge is that although my complaints may be justified, they provide no value other than promoting negativity and damaging morale. Rather than building others up, it is far easier to tear them down and reprimand them for their mistakes. It has taken me years to learn that complaining helps no one. It only adds gasoline to the fire and hinders problem-solving. Therefore, I have had to force myself to learn the discipline of thinking before I speak, because responding is always a wise choice. Reacting merely magnifies immaturity. Therefore, I now aim to guard my tongue before saying or doing something I regret which may hurt others.

Taming the tongue is easier said than done, but our spiritual health is dependent upon our ability to practice self-control over the severity and volatility of our emotions. It is always better to consider the impact our words might have on others before letting them fly out of our mouths unfiltered. It seems relatively easy, but resisting the urge to complain can mean the difference between living in dysfunction and chaos or resting in peaceful contentment. It all depends on how we respond. Therefore, we must think before we speak and measure our words with kindness and consideration to avoid complaining.

Application

1. Since Jesus died to pay your eternal debt, what do you have to complain about in the grand scheme of things?
2. Which circumstances trigger your propensity to complain?
3. Who do you hurt when you start to complain? How so?
4. How is complaining cancerous to those around you?
5. What difference can counting trials as joy have on your ability to resist complaining about them?
6. Have you given others permission to hold you accountable when they hear you starting to complain? Why or why not?
7. Why is it important to remove the log from your own eye before complaining about the foolishness of others?

Prayer

Lord, Your infinite grace is sufficient to meet all my needs, yet I allow my mind to drift away from the blessing of Your sovereign provision. I complain far more than I give thanks. I also struggle making sense of my discontentment. Why am I so self-centered? Why am I not more appreciative of all You have given me? Why do I focus on the imperfections of others when I know I am no better? Convict my self-righteousness, Lord. I cannot continue living this way! Break my foolish pride and help me build others up rather than seeking opportunities to tear them down. I never want to be a cancer of negativity to those around me. I repent of my sins of complaining and pray that You give me wisdom to tame my tongue and measure my words more carefully. Amen.

Day 18 – Contentment

*"And God is able to make all grace abound to you,
so that having all sufficiency in all things at all times,
you may abound in every good work."*

— 2 Corinthians 9:8 —

There is a big difference between wants and needs. For example, we need food, water, clothing, and proper shelter to survive. We do not need anything else if we simplify our lives down to the bare minimum. That is easier said than done in a materialistic culture, though. What makes things difficult is the language we use on a daily basis portrays our wants as non-negotiable needs, yet we do not need the majority of things we possess. They are nice-to-have, not a need-to-have. However, we act as if they are mandatory and then wonder why we feel so discontent and distressed when our desires are not met.

What complicates things further is that we expect God to provide everything our hearts selfishly desire. However, He is not a genie in a bottle and will not settle for being treated as such. Certainly, God loves us and always wants what is best for us, but He sees what we cannot and knows the dangers which lie ahead. He also knows every intimate detail about us, which means He sees the true intentions of our hearts when we chase after worldly pleasures. Therefore, we must learn to trust the Lord rather than ourselves and stop expecting Him to fulfill our laundry list of wishes whenever we want something.

I have learned that sin is never content. It only craves more. The problem is that I once twisted God's holy provision of sex by distorting and devaluing the beauty of His creation. I treated sex as a commodity rather than a gift. For example, my wife is God's greatest treasure to me outside of salvation, and physical intimacy is one of the precious gifts He gives us as a married couple to enjoy. However, when I allowed entitlement and expectation to taint my perspective of sex, it was no longer special. It became something I needed to fuel my ego, feed my flesh, and validate my anxieties. Without personal gratification I felt incomplete, because pleasure had become a false idol I worshipped, not a gift I treasured.

To put it another way, it is sobering to wake up and not remember a thing. When we fill our minds with selfish desires and taint God's sovereign provision, we lose all sense of what is important. Sex, money, power, and possessions are all wants, not needs. If we do not have them, we can still spend our days praising God for all the blessings He has given. The problem is we fail to see how good we truly have it when we look around, compare ourselves to others, and complain about what we lack. If we would count our blessings instead of being unappreciative, we would discover the secret to living peacefully is always praising God for our lot in life.

Contentment is all about being satisfied with the Lord's provision because we see the big picture of our lives from His vantage point. We recognize that we came into this world with nothing and we will leave it emptyhanded when we pass away. Therefore, contentment compels us to stop and praise God for every blessing He graciously provides because we realize how much we do not deserve it. What we actually warrant is God's wrath for our sins, but Jesus died in our place. Therefore, what could we possibly have to complain about? We have been given the gift of salvation through

Christ! Nothing else matters.

Our perspective is often nearsighted. We rarely appreciate what we have until we lose it, which makes contentment such a critical issue to solve in our lives. The challenge is the more we have, the more we stand to lose if God decides to remove His mighty hand of protection over us. We can only live selfishly for so long until God gives us the object of our desires and the consequences which follow. He did so in the wilderness when the Israelites complained about the manna and craved meat instead (Numbers 11), and He will likewise do so for us if we do not appreciate what we have graciously been given.

To think my marriage almost ended due to discontentment is tragic. How could I have been so addicted to lust? Amber is the most beautiful and Godly woman I have ever known, yet I did not appreciate her. It was not until I almost lost her that I began to realize her infinite value. She forgave me when I least deserved it and endured spiritual warfare because of my sins. Though I took her for granted, she was still content with her decision to marry me because I repented before her and God. She kept her vow to love me because of her unwavering faith in Christ, and I am so grateful she gave me a second chance.

We must remember that the key to life is always being content with what we have but never with who we are. What that means is we accept God's provision and our lot in life, for better or worse, but we strive for positive changes in our personal character. Our desire should be to grow in the image and likeness of Jesus Christ, and that inevitably means dying to our love of self and living for righteousness through Christ. **"But godliness with contentment is great gain, for we brought nothing into the world, and we cannot take anything out of the world" (1 Timothy 6:6–7).**

Application

1. What are you discontent with and complain about most?
2. What fuels your frustration and discontentment? What are your trigger points?
3. Why must you always be content with what you have been given (God's provision) but never with who you are?
4. How is godliness with contentment great gain? What was Paul trying to teach Timothy that you need to learn as well?
5. What Gospel are you preaching when you stop complaining?
6. How has your example of discontentment and complaining rubbed off on your family and friends?
7. How can you be more thankful rather than focusing your attention on what you think you need to be happy?

Prayer

Lord, thank You for Your sovereign provision. You have sustained me with far more blessings than I deserve. You meet my needs, though I do not always appreciate it. I confess that I focus more on what I lack than I should. Please forgive me. Help me count my blessings when I wake up each morning rather than looking at life from a glass-half-empty perspective. Your grace is more than sufficient and I want to celebrate Your sovereign provision in every aspect of my life. I pray that others learn to praise You as well based on what they see in me. Help me to continue sharpening my character against the grindstone of Your absolute truth. Make me a better man, Lord. Amen.

Day 19 – Arrogance

> *"Talk no more so very proudly, let not arrogance come from your mouth; for the Lord is a God of knowledge, and by him actions are weighed."*
>
> — 1 Samuel 2:3 —

Does anyone enjoy being around a know-it-all? Not really, if we are being honest, because those who think they know everything are often too busy talking to hear what others have to say. Self-consumed people crave an audience they can enlighten with their wealth of knowledge to solicit praise and adoration. Desire for affirmation fuels their efforts to interject in practically every discussion they find themselves. When their wisdom is not acknowledged, they attempt to force their way into conversations rather than listen to the thoughts and opinions of those who may possess greater knowledge and personal experience.

At the core of a know-it-all attitude is love of self, but arrogance is the fruit which breaks forth from the seed of pride in our hearts. It positions us to believe we are superior to others and fosters conceitedness. No man who displays arrogance is humble enough to recognize those he has trampled upon to exalt himself. He is not concerned with others' interests and opinions because they are insignificant compared to his own. That is often why those who are arrogant lack true friends, because they surround themselves with people who feed their egos rather than those who might hold them accountable to steer them toward humility.

If there is one character attribute Amber sought to break me of when we were first married, it was my know-it-all attitude. It drove her nuts and rightfully so. She would get frustrated and angry when I interrupted her or interjected my thoughts without taking time to listen. I was so concerned with getting my point across that I steamrolled her opinion. I felt that I had all the right answers and knew what I was doing. Why then would she question my skills, knowledge, and experience? I saw it as a lack of faith and trust in me. She viewed it as pride and arrogance and made me aware of it on countless occasions until I woke up and started listening to her advice.

In many ways, arrogance was not an attempt to prop myself above my wife. I was simply defaulting into my old, independent bachelor mode where the only one I trusted was myself. I had been on my own for so long that it was difficult for me to accept that perhaps, I did not have all the answers or that I might be wrong. My heart was far from teachable. I was closed off from accountability. Not even my wife could speak truth into my heart because I thought more highly of my knowledge, personal experience, and abilities than her advice. As a result, conflict in our marriage centered upon my arrogance because I was too stubborn to admit I did not know everything. I quickly learned that her opinion was equal and even more valuable than my own, and that dose of reality humbled my pride immensely.

No one wants to feel like their opinion is worthless. We all desire to be heard and know that our opinion has value, even if it is inaccurate. Closing others off from sharing their blunt and honest opinion can easily promote bitterness and resentment. Therefore, we must guard against propping ourselves up at the expense of others or devaluing their opinion without realizing it. Countless marriages have ended in divorce because wives, especially, feel they are not being heard and that their thoughts and feelings do not matter to their husbands. However, why? What has caused them to come to that unfortunate conclusion other than the arrogant self-righteousness of their husbands?

In many ways, it is because we are unwilling to sit down and hear what they have to say by listening to understand. We may not intend to come across as if we know everything. However, if we are unwilling to hear what our wives have to say or fail to respond to them with gentleness, respect, and consideration, we are devaluing their self-worth and communicating, "I am more important than you." Again, at the crux of conflict in most marriages is a root of pride which elevates love of self at the expense of our brides. Sadly, arrogance is the method we use to communicate our superiority, whether we realize it or not, even though we are called to love, honor, and cherish our wives as Christ does His church.

When Amber first exposed my arrogance, I immediately denied that her assessment was accurate. How could she make such an accusation? Yet the more I looked in the mirror, the more I realized that I was elevating my opinion above hers and hurting her more deeply than I realized. She gave up everything she had marrying me and moving 600-miles away from the only home she had ever known. She had no family or friends close by to lean on except me and all I was doing was crushing her spirit by not listening to what she had to say. Looking back, it is no surprise she battled mild depression our first year of marriage because I completely failed to live with her in an understanding way. I was too focused on myself to attentively guard her heart, and our marriage began on rocky ground because I elevated myself above her which I deeply regret.

Application

1. Do you struggle having a know-it-all attitude? How so?
2. In what ways are you prone to think more highly of yourself than you ought? What fuels your arrogance?
3. When you defy God's Word and yield to temptation, do you see the arrogance of your decision? Why or why not?
4. How is arrogance a precursor to hypocrisy?
5. Why is arrogance so frightening to women? What risks do they take marrying men who think only of themselves?
6. How have you felt being on the receiving end of someone's pride and arrogance? What did you learn?
7. What gifts or talents has God given that you take credit for? Why do you feel a need for personal recognition?

Prayer

Lord, when I look in the mirror, I do not necessarily see an arrogant man staring back at me. I see a man who loves his family. However, actions speak louder than words and my track record is not good. The more I reflect upon the depth and breadth of sinful pride and arrogance in my heart, I am convicted that I have a much bigger problem than I realize. Give me fresh eyes to see the error of my ways and wisdom to change my selfish behavior so that I no longer hurt myself or others. I am nothing without You, but I realize that sometimes I act as if I can somehow live independently from Your grace and succeed. Please forgive my arrogance. I want to glorify You alone because You are worthy to be praised. Amen.

Day 20 – Meekness

> *"He was oppressed, and he was afflicted, yet he opened not his mouth; like a lamb that is led to the slaughter, and like a sheep that before its shearers is silent, so he opened not his mouth."*
>
> — Isaiah 53:7 —

Meekness is not a character attribute we often hear or talk about. If asked to define what it means, most people would struggle giving an accurate answer. What we fail to realize is that meekness was one of Jesus' greatest character traits. How then can we be so ambiguous on what it means if Jesus is our ultimate example? Meekness is about displaying quiet strength and remaining calm under pressure. It is mild-tempered and not easily provoked to anger. It can also endure persecution because it is rooted in submission to God's sovereignty.

Jesus is the perfect example because He was strong as a lion and gentle as a lamb. He possessed extraordinary strength to shoulder the sins of the world yet forgave those who literally nailed Him to the cross. It defies logic how we could love and forgive our enemies like Jesus did. However, meekness is not a hope or suggestion but a command. Therefore, when we love the unlovable and forgive the unforgiveable, we display meekness to a world bent toward anger and restitution. The spiritually lost and broken cannot comprehend such behavior. However, as Christians, we can because our Savior willing died on our behalf to forgive our sins.

When we pay forward the immeasurable grace and mercy of Jesus Christ, we are proclaiming a message the world cannot understand or fathom. Our culture promotes an 'eye for an eye' and 'tooth for a tooth' when we have been hurt or offended, whereas Jesus commands us to love our enemies and pray for those who persecute us. It makes no logical sense to display meekness, if we think about it, except that Christ was the epitome of calm under pressure and submission to the Father's will. In other words, He did not have to die for our sins. He chose to, which teaches us how strong He was not to retaliate but freely accept injustice instead.

I struggle identifying with meekness. I am the type of guy who has no issue holding a grudge against those who have offended me. I can write people off completely. Wounds cut deep and I have used my self-protecting tendencies to divorce myself from those who do not care about my family. We have certainly been persecuted for our faith. I have even written off certain extended family members for their unwillingness to spend time with us despite our efforts to travel and visit them. That is on me, though. I made those decisions to hold grudges rather than forgive and forget, and I will be held accountable by God for my actions if I do not repent of my sin.

What I have learned is the foolish actions of others should not dictate my behavior, for I am led by the Spirit in obedience to Scripture. Therefore, I am without excuse before my Creator if I hold a bitter grudge against others. God will not honor my hardheartedness on judgment day for being calloused and unwilling to show grace, mercy, and forgiveness to those who have rejected me or my family. Yes, I may have legitimate reasons from the world's perspective to be bitter, angry, jealous, or insulted, but God calls me to submit to His will and display meekness rather than arrogance. He expects me to trust His sovereign grace when others revile or persecute our faith in the Gospel of Jesus Christ.

The reason meekness is best described as quiet strength is that it does not seek to defend itself. Rather, it leaves judgment in the hands of God who knows all (Rom. 12:19). It is also strong enough to withstand the flaming arrows of the enemy which attempt to exploit the weaknesses in our spiritual armor. Satan wants nothing more than for us to crack under pressure and throw in the towel on loving those who reject the foundation of our faith. However, when we choose to respond in love when logic says retaliate, we demonstrate to a lost world that there is more power in grace and forgiveness than bitterness and hatred.

Undoubtedly, the Gospel will never reach its full potential to save the lost if we live opposed to the righteous character of Jesus Christ. Our righteous example, or lack thereof, is critical. Therefore, meekness should be our first priority rather than our last resort. We can say we are Christians all we want, but until we apply God's Word, we are not stepping out in faith and allowing the Spirit to work in and through us. God is glorified when we surrender to His authority, obey His holy Word, and submit to His sovereignty, and meekness allows us to do all three simultaneously by the power of the Holy Spirit in Jesus' mighty name.

All we must do is abandon our creature comforts and trust that what God has in store for us far exceeds what we could ask for or imagine. If the blessings which await those who give their lives to Jesus were not worth it, Christianity would have died 2,000 years ago. However, it continued to spread among the nations because Jesus is the Way, the Truth, and the Life. The meekness He showed submitting to the Father and giving His life on the cross is reason enough for us to emulate His example. It simply comes down to living for Him rather than ourselves and being meek like He was.

Application

1. How would you define meekness? What does it practically look like?
2. What makes Jesus the epitome of meekness?
3. Which aspects of your character could be considered meek?
4. Which aspects of your character would benefit mightily from learning and applying meekness?
5. Do you struggle holding grudges and writing people off when you have been hurt or offended? Why or why not?
6. Why is it important to remain calm under pressure? What does it reveal to others about the power of meekness?
7. How can you love your enemies more and bless those who persecute you in Jesus' name?

Prayer

Lord, You have given me the perfect example of meekness when You willingly went to the cross and died for my sins. I cannot fathom what You must have felt shouldering the sins of the world, yet You forgave those who crucified You. I am convicted by how easily anger, bitterness, and resentment have poisoned my heart from loving my enemies. Help me learn from Your example so that You are glorified when I choose to love and not retaliate. I want my life to be a beacon of grace and mercy, and I know that my behavior will draw people to You or pull them away from Your presence. I want to be known as a man who is strong but gentle. Teach me Your ways so I may humbly walk in them forevermore. Amen.

Day 21 – Denial

> *"For we must all appear before the judgment seat of Christ, so that each one may receive what is due for what he has done in the body, whether good or evil."*
>
> — 2 Corinthians 5:10 —

We all have problems. The real question is whether we will admit our failures and do something about them. Denial is one of those character flaw issues which hits us right between the eyes. It forces us to reconcile our rejection of truth and accept that we make poor decisions far too often. Denial is the tuning fork of pride which rings in our hearts when people get a little too close for comfort in our personal business. It means we are not ready to admit our struggles with sin or even talk about them, because we fail to see a need for change. In other words, we believe we are fine just as we are!

Denial magnifies our spiritual immaturity. It is impossible to claim we possess Godly character yet reject the accountability of others who call our sins to attention. Rather, it takes humility to mourn our sins and complete the process of repentance. However, if we are unwilling to hear what others have to say and reject their wisdom, discernment, and counsel, we will never recognize our blind spots or know how to remedy them moving forward. Accountability is truly the heartbeat of our faith in Christ. Without it, we would never see our sins clearly or understand our need for salvation. That is why we must confess our sins and stop denying our problems.

Denial was a constant problem in my past for longer than I care to remember. By allowing half-truths and half-denials to weave interchangeably throughout my life, I struggled maintaining a Biblical standard of black and white regarding sin. Grey was far more flexible and applicable to any given situation, so I proceeded to position my sins as merely temptations rather than a foregone conclusion. Before Amber and I wed, I divulged most of my past sins but failed to admit one which remained an enormous problem. Consequently, I manipulated her into believing my struggles with sexual sin were a thing of the past, not a present battle which mightily consumed my heart and mind at the time.

What ensued was a long battle with hypocrisy where I wore the mask of a righteous man while holding secret sins close to my heart. If I could go back and change one thing, it would be to admit my struggles, confess my sins, and seek professional help. I put Amber through agony for not coming clean before we got married. She would have been better off walking away rather than marrying me. Instead, she has withstood an onslaught of spiritual warfare which has plagued her mind ever since. Even so, she has learned to trust me again because I have chosen to live in the light of accountability and repentance rather than the darkness of secrecy and deceit.

Denial does us no favors. It only makes matters worse. It also does us no good to admit we have issues and make little to no effort changing them. We cannot act as if we have done enough to fix our problems when privately, we know we have not. Countless men, myself included, have successfully melded confession and denial into a strategic weapon to manipulate others into thinking we have recognized the error of our ways. However, though we may believe we have evaded accountability, God stands poised to punish our souls if we do not repent of our sins and live for righteousness.

For if we refuse to confess our sins and humble ourselves, we will be judged by God severely. Denial cannot exist in the heart of a righteous man who is committed to honesty and integrity. Therefore, we must act in good faith and stop our wickedness if we desire for the Lord to extend grace, mercy, and pardon for our sins. Jesus warned those who reveled in their religious hypocrisy, **"You are of your father the devil, and your will is to do your father's desires. He was a murderer from the beginning, and does not stand in the truth, because there is no truth in him. When he lies, he speaks out of his own character, for he is a liar and the father of lies" (John 8:44)**. Therefore, when we look in the mirror, who or what do we see?

I know how it feels to stand on opposite ends of the honesty vs. denial spectrum. I became dangerously proficient at hiding from guilt, shame, and regret. Without accountability, it was easy to justify my sins rather than remedy them. However, I had to stop lying about my struggles to God and others and own how out of control my sins had become. In retrospect, no man wants to admit he can no longer discern right from wrong, but I could not distinguish truth from a lie. I believed everything and everyone around me caused me to sin and that justification held me captive for many years.

Regrettably, I had all the self-validation I needed to say and do whatever I wanted without the slightest consideration of others. It did not matter who I hurt in the process. Denial was simply a means to an end. However, that train of thought inevitably brought me to my knees when Amber was on the verge of Biblically divorcing me. I finally knew I had to change. Thankfully, I stopped hiding from the truth and stepped into the light which ultimately restored my broken marriage. However, it could have easily ended altogether had I kept denying that I had a problem in the first place.

Application

1. Do you struggle admitting you have an addiction to sin? Why or why not?
2. What are your biggest fears owning your sins and walking in the light of God's truth?
3. What should self-denial look like in the life of a Christian?
4. What scars do you bear which testify to a time you refused to admit you were enslaved to sin?
5. How can you humble yourself more and confess your sins?
6. Whose accountability means the most to you? How can you seek wise counsel more often?
7. What do you stand to lose when you hide your sins and fail to admit you are struggling with temptation?

Prayer

Lord, it goes without saying that when I yield to the lusts of my flesh, I deny the truth of Your Word and exchange it for a lie. I cannot continue believing that somehow I can walk in the shadows of deception without being held accountable for my actions on judgment day. The enemy has convinced me that I am justified to yield to my fleshly desires because unfortunate circumstances and other people are to blame for my actions. I now see the foolishness of my thinking and repent of my naïve denial. I know that I need to change but am scared of what the future holds if I humble myself and seek counsel. Therefore, give me courage to walk in the light of Your truth and embrace self-denial so I can fix my sin issues. Amen.

Day 22 - Ownership

"I acknowledged my sin to you, and I did not cover my iniquity; I said, 'I will confess my transgressions to the LORD,' and you forgave the iniquity of my sin."

— Psalm 32:5 —

There is a monumental difference between making a mistake and committing a sin. A mistake is a decision which produces a negative result that we did not intend. For instance, if a ball is thrown and accidentally hits someone, or if a glass is knocked over and spills on the table, it is obvious that mistakes were made. Truly, mistakes are unintentional, meaning their purpose is never to maliciously hurt anyone, even though negative results may occur. We all make mistakes, but they have less to do with our hearts because they are accidental rather than intentional. They simply come to fruition despite our best intentions to keep them from happening.

Sins are completely different. We know what we are doing when we sin because disobeying God's Word is a volitional choice. We act according to our own free will which magnifies the implications of choosing to fail. Sin is a conscious decision to rebel against the Lord's command and satisfy fleshly desires. We do not accidently fall into sin. Rather, we put ourselves in positions and environments which are conducive for mischief, rebellion, and disobedience. Thus, we yield to temptation instead of resisting it. The problem is we do not want to admit that sins are a choice because we would rather evade personal responsibility altogether.

This is where the battle between ownership and denial takes center stage. It is much easier to justify our sins and blame shift responsibility than accept accountability. Ownership compels us to proactively confess to the crimes we have committed. Denial simply provides an escape route to avoid the consequences of our actions and continue living in sin, without the slightest care for who we hurt in the process or whatever happens next. It all comes down to intentionality and determining whether we find our treasure in the pleasures of this world or the truth of God's Word in relationship to Jesus Christ.

I did not grow up with a silver spoon in my mouth. Far from it! I had to work hard to support myself and pay my own way as a full-time college student. Making money was never easy, but I worked as a commission salesman to pay my bills and build up some savings. However, the desire to get rich quick was incredibly tempting. For instance, one night while I was watching television, an infomercial caught my eye. It was the prototypical pyramid scheme, but I was a college student and too naïve to know better. Foolishly, I called the number on the screen, signed a waiver, gave them my shipping info, and spent my life's savings on health supplements which I assumed were the golden ticket to riches and success.

It only took a few days, but I realized I had made a horrible lapse in judgment and there was no way to get my money back. The fine print of the contract I signed cleared the company of all liability and I was completely broke with nothing to show for it. Devastation overwhelmed me. How could I have been so stupid? I wanted to blame the company but no one forced my hand. I made the reckless decision. Therefore, I was solely responsible for the consequences which ensued because I failed to seek the wisdom and counsel of others. I coveted the ease and comfort of success. It had become an idol in my heart and would not be satisfied until I took a risk and gave in to temptation. Regrettably, I made a horrible judgment call.

I learned a hard lesson from that experience which revolved around owning my personal decisions rather than pointing the finger. I could have easily blamed the company who took advantage of me, but again, they did not force me to sign on the dotted line. I chose to buy into their deception which meant, for better or worse, I owned the consequences of my actions without excuse. Denying my foolishness would have been pointless. Thus, I accepted my fate and asked God to forgive me so I could learn from my poor choice and never make the same bad decision again.

The key to ownership is not being baited into believing we can share personal responsibility. When we allow our minds to assume that 99.9% is the same as 100%, we leave the door cracked open to blame shift or justify our sins instead of accepting full responsibility. Opportunity will always be readily available, if we desire, to play the victim card and appease our flesh. However, we cannot drink that deadly poison. Rather, we must own our decisions. Therefore, the only way to truly learn from our mistakes is to declare, "Lord, I own my sins. 100%. No one forced my hand. I chose to sin and I fully accept the consequences of my actions. Discipline me as You see fit so I can learn from my foolish lapse in judgment."

If our hearts maintain that attitude and perspective, we will learn from our poor choices and decrease the likelihood of repeating them. That is not a guarantee, of course, but it does give us the greatest opportunity to guard our hearts and minds from temptation going forward. Denying we have a sin problem only prolongs the inevitable. However, ownership breaks the chain of bondage in our minds and charts our hearts on a new course towards repentance, forgiveness, and lasting freedom in Christ.

Application

1. Why is there freedom in ownership and bondage in denial?
2. When it comes to ownership of your sins, why is 99.9% vastly different than 100%? Why is 100% critical to heart change?
3. Why are blame shifting and justification the same as denial?
4. What happens if you confess your sins but do not fully repent of them?
5. What difference does it make to own the consequences of your sins and not fight them?
6. How has God delivered you from the chains of sinful idols through ownership and repentance?
7. Do you label your foolish actions as sins or mistakes? Why? What difference does it make?

Prayer

Lord, You know my heart much better than I and see through the façade of my blame shifting and justification. Why I struggle to admit I am sinner when it comes to owning my poor choices makes no sense. The only one I am fooling is myself! Help me recognize my failures as You see them and embrace Biblical repentance so I can find freedom in the truth of Your Word. You are far more gracious and merciful to me than I deserve and I thank You for Your unending love and patience. Help me to never take advantage of the cross but to bow before it daily in humble surrender and submission. Cleanse my rebellious heart and wash my mind from thinking I can survive worldly temptations on my own. Amen.

Day 23 – Insecurity

> *"For you formed my inward parts; you knitted me together in my mother's womb. I praise you, for I am fearfully and wonderfully made. Wonderful are your works; my soul knows it well."*
>
> — Psalm 139:13-14 —

We all struggle with uncertainty to one degree or another. Insecurity is one of those issues which magnifies our lack of faith and trust in God who made us just the way we are for a specific plan and purpose. It is an area where we question God's sovereignty as it relates to our lot in life or the hand we have been dealt which seems difficult to bear. Insecurity often fuels our fears and anxieties because we struggle knowing how to reconcile the past, understand the present, and predict the future. Moreover, it compels us to be more self-reliant than we should and doubt God's ability to help us overcome things that worry us most.

Anxiety does us no favors, which is why Scripture speaks so much about it. **"Do not be anxious about anything, but in everything by prayer and supplication with thanksgiving let your requests be made known to God" (Philippians 4:6).** What Paul addresses is not just the need to die to anxiety, but to release our worries back to God through prayer and worship. In other words, communication with the Lord is paramount to overcome our insecurities by sharing with Him what is on our hearts, both good and bad. Granted, He already knows what we are thinking and feeling, but that is not the point. It is all about casting our cares upon

Him rather than hiding our thoughts and feelings in isolation.

Insecurity directly impacts contentment as well. How can we sleep peacefully if we are constantly looking at life from a glass-half-empty lens? How can we be thankful if we are always focused on what is wrong or absent from our lives? Insecurities leave us vulnerable to attack by the enemy because we are left paralyzed by fear. Rather than working to shore up our defense and fix the cracks in our spiritual armor, we simply freeze and focus all attention on our inability to guard our minds. The truth is that apart from Christ, we cannot protect ourselves. We need the power of the Holy Spirit to fight on our behalf and in our defense. However, we must be actively seeking His help, not passively succumbing to fear, and giving up altogether.

My greatest area of insecurity centers around whether I am truly loved, respected, and desired by my wife. Amber is my most trusted friend and the one I look to for affirmation daily. Unfortunately, that puts a tremendous amount of pressure on her to be perfect, because I often blame her for when I am in a foul mood. I allow her actions to dictate mine, which enables me to point the finger rather than accept responsibility for my actions. If she is having a rough day or struggling with self-control, I allow her behavior to impact my temperament. Moreover, I self-funnel what she is thinking and feeling and make it about me, which only fuels my insecurity and plunges me into paranoia and despair.

Realistically, Amber will never fulfill my needs the way God can, nor should I place that unrealistic expectation upon her to always be perfect. My actions cannot be contingent upon her behavior because personal insecurity is my cross to bear, not hers. She cannot be my scapegoat to avoid responsibility either. I must own my self-doubt and stop expecting her actions to always dictate mine. Rather,

I must protect my marriage by not expecting her to always solve my need for love, respect, and intimacy. Her greatest blessing is holding me accountable to God's Word and encouraging me to rely on Jesus to fulfill the deepest longings of my heart. In other words, her God-given role is to love and support me as the Spirit guides and directs, not as I selfishly will.

When we look to other people or the things of this world to pacify our insecurities, we demonstrate how little we trust God to meet our needs. Keep in mind, we were known by God long before we were created in our mother's womb. Why then would we doubt the sovereignty of His creation? If we have physical limitations or psychological handicaps, do we fail to believe God has a specific plan and purpose for the trials and difficulties we face? If we have suffered pain and trauma as innocent victims of torment and abuse, are we not comforted that God will judge mankind according to their deeds and vindicate our suffering?

Sometimes, the insecurities we face are the result of factors outside our sphere of influence or control, but that does not mean God cannot redeem our souls and bring forth beauty from ashes. For our ultimate identity is not in past sins or present trials, but in the hope of salvation we have been given by grace through faith in Jesus Christ. No matter what we struggle with this side of heaven, if we are born-again into God's family, our insecurities have been divinely redeemed because Jesus rose from the grave and defeated sin and death once and for all. Therefore, we no longer need to carry the scarlet letter of self-doubt as a badge of honor. Instead, we can lay our fears, doubts, and anxieties at the foot of the cross where our Savior died in our place to pay our ransom and free us from sin's bondage.

Application

1. What specifically are you most insecure about?
2. How do anxiety and insecurity go hand-in-hand? How do they influence one another?
3. When you look in the mirror, what insecurities do you often struggle with? Why do you allow them to bother you?
4. How can the Lord be glorified in your weakness?
5. What has God taught you about depending upon His grace through the insecurities you harbor deep inside your heart?
6. What are the dangers of looking to others rather than God to solve your insecurities?
7. How can you begin to praise God for your imperfections rather than complain about what you lack?

Prayer

Lord, I am fearfully and wonderfully made, yet I struggle to see how my shortcomings and imperfections are a blessing. I realize my perspective is often shortsighted because my mind is focused on insecurities which make me think less of myself. I know I should praise You for my weaknesses and count my trials as joy, but I struggle seeing the silver-lining of Your grace in my suffering. Help me reject the lies Satan continues to whisper and embrace Your Holy Word instead. I may not see it now, but I trust You will reveal what I need to know to survive another day in this fallen world. I place my hope in You, Lord, knowing Your grace is my delight and my reward. Thank you for giving me eternal security. Amen.

Day 24 - Protection

"The Lord is my shepherd; I shall not want. He makes me lie down in green pastures. He leads me beside still waters. He restores my soul. He leads me in paths of righteousness for his name's sake."

— Psalm 23:1-3 —

There is so much in the world to be concerned about these days, but none of it will matter when we stand before God on judgment day and Christ's blood covers our iniquities. Jesus paid the ultimate price to atone for the penalty of our sins and secure our salvation. It was the ultimate sacrifice of love and devotion, which means we have received the greatest gift of protection we could ever hope for. Eternity awaits us, not because of anything we have done to deserve it but because of saving grace. That is why we can rejoice with the angels, for we have victory in Jesus who washed our sins away.

Knowing this, how can we protect our hearts from yielding to fear, doubt, and worry (just to name a few)? If Jesus paid it all, why do we allow insecurities to plague our minds and make us anxious? Christ's death, burial, and resurrection are sufficient to give us the security we need to trust His sovereignty every day of our lives. Why then do we doubt Him? Protection seems like just a physical issue, but it pales in comparison to the spiritual realm where battles rage within our minds. The enemy is always searching for weaknesses in our armor. Therefore, we must continually guard our minds from all sides and every angle to avoid succumbing to evil.

What every man wants to know is how to protect himself better. It may seem like an easy task, but protection demands we make bold changes and perform behavioral amputation, if necessary. Sin is like cancer. It spreads discreetly but rapidly. Most often, we have no clue we are terminally sick until our behavior becomes so destructive that the cancer of sin makes its presence known. At that point, surgery is required to save our lives from spiritual ruin. That is why the Great Surgeon stands poised and ready to heal our souls. However, we must allow Him full access to our hearts so that He can remove the eternal stain of rebellion before it is too late.

One thing God has taught me is to distinguish between fruit and root if I desire to overcome sin in my life. Logic says if I struggle with lust, then I need to identify the trigger points, which fuel my fleshly desires, and put an end to them. However, I miss the point if I believe sexual immorality is my ultimate problem. It is merely the fruit of a far deeper sin issue called love of self. My selfishness is the ultimate root cause which provides the means necessary (i.e. nutrients) to satisfy my appetite. In my case, sexual self-gratification was how my sin manifested itself. It was the fruit of my desire but not the root issue. Far beneath the surface was an evil intent to please myself at all cost.

When we come to realize that we have been focusing on the wrong problem the whole time, it is demoralizing and freeing to our psyche. We regret the amount of time and energy we wasted trying to fix our spiritual problems with band-aids instead of surgical equipment. However, it is also liberating to know the root cause of our failed efforts to change. Sadly, we know what it feels like to try and fix our sin issues only to revert back to them with relative ease. Ironically, our behavior is also the definition of insanity—doing the same thing over and over and expecting different results.

What God wants us to learn more than anything is that protecting our hearts and minds supersedes everything. To be a Godly spiritual leader, we must reconcile our sin issues at the root level so we do not become a stumbling block to others. We are also provided opportunities to model righteousness in our homes by filtering out cultural influences which wage war against the truth of God's Word. Satan is always looking for a way to infiltrate our homes through bad habits, hobbies, and personal interests, which in today's selfish culture, centers on electronics and social media.

My wife and I have been intentional to protect our home by not allowing the enemy to fill our daughters' hearts and minds with garbage. For example, we cancelled our cable and began streaming networks to pick and choose what we watch on television. Our girls had to wait till they were fifteen to have their own smartphone. We have limited social media usage to a minimum, implemented curfews on screen time, resisted all videogaming, and scrutinized movies so we are not welcoming evil into our home. Certainly, we have made mistakes along the way, but we have also drastically reduced the amount of entry points for sin to negatively influence our faith in Christ.

In the end, protection is all about guarding our hearts so we can positively influence others to do likewise. We cannot teach others what we do not personally know and fail to apply in our own lives. Hypocrisy flourishes when we act as if we know what we are doing when nothing could be further from the truth. Our actions can contradict our words, if we are not careful, which is a serious problem. Therefore, protecting those we love is contingent upon us first guarding our hearts and minds from spiritual warfare to avoid being judgmental and hypocritical.

Application

1. Why is spiritual protection greater than physical protection?
2. Where are you most vulnerable to temptation? Why?
3. Are you more focused on the fruit of your sin or the root cause of your selfishness? How so?
4. Which type of protection (physical, emotional, spiritual, or psychological) is harder for you to apply?
5. What changes have you made to protect your heart and mind? If none, what changes can you begin making?
6. How has God shielded you from greater consequences than your sins actually produced?
7. Why is the blood of Jesus your ultimate protection?

Prayer

Lord, protection is not something I often think about. I tend to be on autopilot and focus on the things which are right in front of me. I know the mind is where spiritual warfare takes place, but I do not pay enough attention to it as I should. I have allowed the enemy easy access to my heart because my mind is not fully guarded. I have focused on the fruit of my sin rather than the root of my selfishness, and I feel just as enslaved to sin and temptation as ever before. Help me die to my love of self and invest time and energy cleansing my mind with Your absolute truth. Inspire me to plant a flag in my home that honors You. Help me remove temptations so they do not become a stumbling block to my family. I long to protect those I love, so give me courage to face the enemy by Your Word. Amen.

Day 25 - Callousness

"They have become callous and have given themselves up to sensuality, greedy to practice every kind of impurity."

— Ephesians 4:19 —

If there is one issue most men identify with, it would be our propensity toward callousness. In many ways, callousness is often identified as insensitivity, which may or may not be true. On the whole, men are not wired like women. We are emotional, but how we express our feelings looks different compared to women. It is not that we are insensitive. We just tend to be matter of fact, blunt, and straight to the point, more often than not. Some of us are also analytical, which means we can be logical or emotionally disengaged at times. However, there are distinct advantages to tempering our feelings and not being controlled by them.

The challenge is that men tend to lean toward callousness when empathy and compassion are required. Without knowing it, we can convey to others that we are coldhearted towards their needs and indifferent to their struggles. Many of us easily fall victim to callousness because our perceived disinterest somehow gets lost in translation. People also tend to judge a book by its cover. So, if our receptivity to others appears apathetic, they will likely walk away because they assume we care very little for who they are, what they think, or the trials they might be facing.

I love shepherding discipleship groups. The opportunities God has provided to lead so many men through **"Wilderness Survival"** have been an honor and privilege. Discussion is rarely soft and vague. Guys tend to tell it like it is and rarely filter what flies out of their mouths in the presence of other men. I always encourage them to be authentic in my group—raw, brash, blunt, and honest, because I am far less concerned with the outside of the cup than what is inside. I just want them to be vulnerable so they can embrace who God made them and stop apologizing for being innately male. Case in point: Jesus was a strong, manly carpenter. He did manual labor all the time. Therefore, what makes us think we cannot be manly too and embrace the uniqueness of who God made us?

For better or worse, callousness is a part of who I am. My wife cannot stand my insensitivity at times, but she has learned to see the benefits and detriments. My goal is simply to maintain my calloused demeanor in crises and emergency situations and die to it when sensitivity is required. It is a delicate balance because there are pros and cons to each. For example, being callous allowed me to keep calm when I had my heart attack and even crack jokes with staff members when I was in the hospital. However, there have been times when callousness has communicated insensitivity to my family when they were hurting and needed a gentle shoulder to cry on.

The key is understanding how dangerous callousness can be when others do not know the true intent of our hearts. Case in point, I had a man in one of my survival groups confess that his son never knew he could be emotional because of his military history. All his son saw was callousness devoid of emotion, packaged in a tough as nails, armed forces exterior. It was not until my friend let his guard down and allowed God to break the emotional walls he had developed over time that his father-son relationship turned the corner. All it took was him embracing humility and allowing the Spirit to radically change his heart.

As men, we tend to think we cannot shed a tear, but that is a lie. Jesus was the manliest guy who ever lived, but He was not afraid to expose the compassion in His heart. Remember that upon arriving at the tomb of Lazarus, **"Jesus wept" (Luke 11:35)**. He did not simply shed a tear in private or stuff his emotions. He physically expressed His emotions publicly. Jesus certainly maintained His composure plenty of times, but in that moment, He let His emotions flow freely. He did what our culture today warns men not to do—cry! However, it was His ability to let down His guard which makes Him that much more relatable to us.

Keep in mind, being calloused does not mean we could care less. We may be harboring our emotions for legitimate reasons to not make a difficult situation worse. However, there comes a point when we must die to our macho persona and soften our hearts to express our emotions. The world needs more Godly men who have wisdom to discern when to toughen up and when to let down their guard. However, most guys are hesitant or unwilling to take that chance, because they are afraid of ridicule, persecution, or being ostracized for their sensitivity.

Truly, most men struggle knowing how to express their emotions, but that is why God made men and women different and created marriage in the first place. We can learn from our wives, mothers, sisters, and friends on how to share what we are thinking and feeling. We just need to humble ourselves and ask for help. Again, callousness is not necessarily a bad thing in every situation. It can also be a valuable asset in the proper environment if channeled correctly. However, if we want to exhibit the attributes of a Godly man, we must guard against callousness which comes across as coldhearted apathy and insensitivity towards the needs of others.

Application

1. In your mind, what does a calloused man look like? What are his defining characteristics?
2. How would you consider your callousness an asset rather than a liability?
3. In what ways have you become calloused to temptation and sin in your life?
4. Think of a time when your callousness was misinterpreted as indifferent, coldhearted, or insensitive. How did that make you feel? What did you learn as a result?
5. How can you learn to express your feelings and emotions rather than putting up an emotional wall towards others?
6. How does isolation often promote callousness in men?

Prayer

Lord, You made me who I am as a man. Thank You for blessing me with the opportunity to be a spiritual leader and a model for righteous behavior in my home. I confess I am not often successful at expressing my thoughts and feelings. It is far easier for me to isolate and put up a psychological wall to hide my true feelings. However, I realize how unhealthy and debilitating that truly is. Help me learn from Your example and the Godly women You have graciously placed in my life. Give me wisdom and discernment to learn from how they express emotion so I can learn from their example. I want to be a more sensitive man and not succumb to fear which tempts me to hide my emotions. Thus, make me more like You, Jesus. Amen.

Day 26 – Compassion

"But if anyone has the world's goods and sees his brother in need, yet closes his heart against him, how does God's love abide in him?"

— 1 John 3:17 —

Compassion is one of the defining character traits of Jesus Christ. Wherever the crowds followed, He had compassion on them because their pain and suffering were immense. **"When he went ashore he saw a great crowd, and he had compassion on them, because they were like sheep without a shepherd" (Mark 6:34)**. In other words, Jesus was aware of His environment, recognized the trials of those He met, and sought to meet their greatest needs because He had the power and authority to do so. He put love into action and changed the world in the process.

Consequently, how aware are we of those whom God has placed in our lives? Do we see them? Like a homeless man panhandling on the street corner, do we recognize his value before God as equal to our own, or do we dismiss him as unworthy of our time, energy, and resources? If we are honest, we do not want to be bothered. Busyness has overwhelmed our schedules to the point where we have little time available to invest into those we love, let alone spare a minute to anyone else in need. We just assume someone else will pick up the slack and step up in our place. However, we miss out on a prime opportunity to be the hands and feet of Jesus when we reject serving others.

Years ago, my family attended a church which sought to alleviate the needs of the community by giving people a chance to use their resources to bless others. Two bulletin boards were placed in the building's entryway with notecards and push pins. All people had to do was humble themselves and ask for help by writing their request, providing their contact #, and posting it on the "needs" board. From there, it was in the hands of the congregation to review the prayer requests and act as the Spirit prompted. Once the action was completed, the notecards were put on the "needs met" board so we could rejoice at what God had done.

The response was overwhelming. People found babysitters, caregivers, employment opportunities, and counsel. Needs for monthly rent, appliances, clothing, and even vehicles were provided free of charge. It was a chance for the body of Christ to step up and put faith into action, and people did so with joy in their hearts to help others less fortunate and struggling. All that was required was to see a need and meet it as the Lord inspired, and hundreds of people were helped because church members stopped thinking only of themselves and started looking out for the interests of others.

Compassion is an opportunity for us to humble ourselves. It forces us to walk a mile in someone's shoes and experience life's hardships from their unique perspective. It convicts us to appreciate what God has provided rather than complain about what we lack. Moreover, it compels our hearts to respond in love and share our time, energy, and resources with others who desperately need help. Therefore, we should not be concerned with gaining anything for our efforts except the satisfaction of giving from the abundance of blessings God has provided us.

Being compassionate can be difficult for men. In many ways, empathy does not come naturally to us because we are not emotionally wired like women. Our heart strings tend to be more calloused than sensitive. However, that does not mean we lack the ability to be compassionate. Just as we might need help learning how to express our emotions, we are just as vulnerable to displaying insensitivity and disinterest when empathy and kindness are required. That is one major reason why women compliment us so well, because they see what we do not and compensate for our emotional deficiencies.

Being a husband and father of four daughters is one of God's greatest blessings to me. I have learned so much from their ability to express thoughts and emotions effectively. Being in sales, I have never struggled with communicating my feelings, yet sometimes I fail miserably at softening my words and having compassion on those who receive my raw and blunt honesty. I can recall moments where I have raised my voice to get my daughters' attention and brought them to tears in the process. It does not take much to emotionally hurt those I care about most. Therefore, I must always consider my words with compassion to ensure they are not lost in translation when I express them.

There is no shame admitting that compassion might be a struggle for us, but the real question is whether we care to do anything about it. We simply cannot say we are compassionate and kind and not back it up with our actions. Therefore, will we throw our hands in the air and declare, "I'm sorry! That's just the way I am!" or humble ourselves and learn how to be more sensitive towards the needs of others? God expects us to be tender-hearted men who sacrifice personal comforts for the greater good. If we cannot, then we are truly no better than unbelievers who care nothing about Jesus or His Gospel of salvation. Compassion requires action, not just good intention and we are expected by God to love others like Jesus.

Application

1. What does it mean to be compassionate and tenderhearted?
2. Are tears a sign of strength or weakness? How so?
3. How can you begin looking out for the interests of others rather than yourself? Who can you begin with first?
4. What is the danger of speaking absolute truth without love and compassion?
5. What are some practical ways you can share the abundance of your possessions with others?
6. What risks do you take when you withhold compassion from those you love?
7. What made Jesus so compassionate? What can you learn from His example?

Prayer

Lord, I am amazed by how compassionate You were to so many people during Your three-year ministry. Your heart was always outwardly focused and attentive to needs all around You. I desire to be a man who is equally sensitive to the Spirit's prompting as well. You have blessed me beyond measure, yet I often forget that I am a steward of Your abundance, not my own. Help me seek opportunities where I can step outside my comfort zone and be Your hands and feet to those who are in desperate need of kindness. Compassion does not come very easily to me. Therefore, help me overcome my discomfort and seek unique opportunities to bless others so that Your holy name may be glorified for eternity. Amen.

Day 27 – Anger

> *"Know this, my beloved brothers: let every person be quick to hear, slow to speak, slow to anger; for the anger of man does not produce the righteousness of God."*
>
> — James 1:19–20 —

Anger is an issue for most men. Due to our impulsive, aggressive, and destructive nature, anger fits our natural temperament like a glove. It is comfortable and familiar. It can also be used as a weapon to inflict great harm if we desire. Whether we realize it, anger is an emotional filter men predominately use to communicate their thoughts and feelings. Granted, anger can be righteous, which is allowed by God when evil or injustice is present. Jesus overturning the tables of the moneychangers in the temple is a prime example (Matt. 21:12-13). However, in most circumstances, anger can be our greatest adversary because it can spread like wildfire and destroy everything in its path if we do not learn to control its unquenchable rage and fury.

The challenge is while most of us know we struggle with anger issues, few attempt to address the problem head-on and solve it once and for all. Ignoring it is pointless. That only makes things worse because denial breeds hypocrisy. Giving up is not an option either because waiving the white flag of surrender only proves our immaturity. No, the only way to combat anger is to maintain self-control, which is easier said than done when we do not know how to filter our emotions properly. Perhaps that is why God's Word has so much to say on the issue because of the severity in which we struggle yielding to our tempers.

Scripture warns us to turn away from unrighteous anger because it is far too easy to be controlled by it. **"Whoever is slow to anger has great understanding, but he who has a hasty temper exalts folly (Proverbs 14:29).** God expects us to use self-control and quell any temptation to react angrily by pausing and responding instead. Keep in mind, reactions are instantaneous. Whatever enters our mind exits through our mouth simultaneously, for better or worse. However, responses are different. When we respond, we pause to think before we speak and weigh the consequences and residual impact of our words before they are uttered.

Responding is our accountability filter which allows us to choose what happens next. James 3 warns that the tongue is a consuming fire of unrighteousness. It only takes a single ember to set a forest ablaze, so we must be wise and understand how powerful and destructive our tongues can be if not wielded properly. Too many men have sent shrapnel into their hearts of their loved ones because they could not control their anger. That truth should convict us with reverent fear. For the Lord will judge those who allow their anger to consume them, and we are vulnerable to judgment if we do not display self-control and learn how to express our emotions in a more healthy manner.

In a marriage conference Amber and I attended many years ago, Dr. Gary Rosberg made an assertion from years of Biblical counseling that men typically filter all their emotions through anger. We may be feeling tired, frustrated, disappointed, or depressed, but anger is the filter we use for whatever emotion we might be feeling in the moment. In other words, anger may not be intended, but that is how it comes across to our loved ones when we struggle articulating how we feel and default to it. At first, I bristled at the notion until I took a hard look in the mirror and recognized how poorly I had been communicating emotions to my wife. He was exactly right! I too fell victim to using anger as my emotional filter in most situations and the frequent conflict in our marriage at the time proved he was correct.

Dr. Rosberg challenged us that day to tap into the greatest resource God created to help us fix our issues: women. That nugget of wisdom was a turning point for me and our marriage. I stopped looking at my wife as the enemy and started appreciating her as God's blessing to teach me how to express my emotions more effectively. Undoubtedly, Amber holds me accountable to the truth of God's Word and calls out when I fail to use self-control. Granted, I have not perfected my ability to resist anger in all situations. That dragon rears its head and spits fire despite my attempts to stop it. However, I have greater self-awareness and recognition of my behavior now to respond with wisdom and discernment before reacting in anger.

The last thing we want to do is strike fear into those we love. No one should ever walk on eggshells around us to avoid our explosions of rage. That is not a healthy environment to live in but one which has the potential for abuse of many kinds if we are not careful. Therefore, it is critical we think before we speak and ensure the words which pour out from our mouths are meant for blessing others rather than cursing. Scripture warns, **"A hot-tempered man stirs up strife, but he who is slow to anger quiets contention" (Proverbs 15:18)**. In other words, we must not only control our temper but seek to understand the reasons why we revert to anger in the first place. For a wise man is not only capable of controlling his anger but displays self-control so that others are not caught in the line of fire.

Application

1. Would you consider yourself an angry man at times? Why or why not?
2. What typically triggers your outbursts of anger?
3. How do you discern between righteous and sinful anger in your behavior? Where is the line in the sand drawn?
4. How do you filter non-angry emotions through anger?
5. Has someone you love ever confronted your unrighteous anger? How did you react or respond?
6. What are the dangers of not extinguishing the fires of sinful anger in your heart?
7. What angers the Lord that you should be angry about too?

Prayer

Lord, while I do not want to admit I struggle with anger, the way I speak to those around me testifies that I lack self-control. My temper can get the best of me even when I try to not lose my cool. Help me learn how to effectively express my thoughts and feelings without defaulting to sinful anger as my universal filter. I do not want to burn a bridge with those I love by reacting when I should be responding. I long to be a righteous example for my family of peace and holiness, and model gentleness instead of rage. Please expose areas of my life which trigger irritated reactions so I can honor You with my words and bless others by bridling my tongue. I have much to learn, but with Your wisdom, I can control my unrighteous anger once and for all. Amen.

Day 28 - Peace

"And let the peace of Christ rule in your hearts, to which indeed you were called in one body. And be thankful."

— Colossians 3:15 —

Those of us who are husbands and fathers know how precious peace and quiet are in the home. Peace is hard to come by when we start building our families, because chaos tends to ensue when more people live under the same roof. Regardless, we do not necessarily have to be a husband or father to appreciate the importance of relational harmony and solitude. Christ proved how critical quiet time with the Father was for His spiritual refreshment. The Gospels detail many occasions where Jesus frequently ventured off on His own to pray and reflect. Therefore, we must be just as eager to carve out time in our daily schedules to get our minds right with the Lord if we expect to be useful doing His work.

When we are consumed with busyness, spiritual disciplines such as Bible study, prayer, and fasting are withdrawn and reprioritized. In other words, they are moved to the bottom of our priority list in favor of functional duties which seem more immediate. We rationalize in our minds that God is not going anywhere, so we will catch up with Him later. What happens, though, when our quality time with God is reduced from every day to every week or month? Do we realize that our lives are in disarray because our souls are malnourished? At what point will we begin to see the forest through the trees and repent of our busyness?

We have all used the excuse, "I don't have time," but is that true? No, it is a lie! We all have the same 24-hours in a day to pick and choose how we will spend our time. Therefore, it is not an issue of quantity but priority that we struggle with. It calls into question where our treasure lies because it is far easier to make excuses than call out our sins. We all want to be used by God, but in full transparency, our priorities are all in disarray. We tend to revolve our lives around the false gods of sport and extracurricular activities to the detriment of spiritual formation in the home. How can this be? Did God not say, **"You shall have no other gods before me" (Exodus 20:3)**?

Oftentimes, the reason we are so restless and discontent is because we have jammed too much busyness into our lives and feel overwhelmed by stress trying to manage it all. Peace is virtually unattainable in such an environment. Therefore, we must clean house and eliminate things which draw us away from God. That is not to say change is easy. On paper, everything seems important. However, if we consider how much time we waste following cultural trends and worldly pleasures, we will soon realize we have far more time available than we realize. We will also discover why quality time with God is so important to maintain our emotional, psychological, and spiritual sanity.

Amber and I have always guarded our family time and limited the number of activities our girls were involved in so we were not enslaved to after-school schedules. Case in point, our teens chose dance as their extracurricular outlet and did so for roughly eight years, which was fairly manageable for our family. They excelled in many styles of dance but finally chose to invest their time and energy in clogging. We traveled a few weekends for competitions and our girls finally competed at nationals, winning a team championship.

Actually, they won every competition they competed in, reaching the pinnacle of success in their first-year of competitive clogging. However, life changed in an instant when my physical health took a turn for the worst.

When I had my heart attack, God taught my family a valuable lesson that tomorrow is not guaranteed. As a result, we reflected on what happened to me and made a collective, family decision. Considering the time and cost associated with traveling and competing, coupled with hospital bills from my surgery, we chose to walk away from dance. Those who knew us were shocked by our decision. Why walk away at the peak of success when we could win more? However, the decision was fairly easy. Faith and family were higher priorities, and our teens wanted to invest more time in ministry growing their faith. Living for applause and a trophy was irrelevant compared to life and death scenarios. Thus, we had peace in our decision because God was our central focus, and we have not regretted that decision since we walked away.

Peace is not some euphoric dream with little chance of becoming reality. We can achieve peace and promote it as well, but we must handle our business and realign our priorities if we expect to be content. Going against the cultural grain and carving out quiet time with the Lord each day is paramount. Honoring Christ must be the central focus of every decision we make. Otherwise, we are prone to worshipping false idols and expecting them to satisfy our souls, which they cannot. Peace is only attainable when we surrender our hearts to the Lord and allow His Spirit to reign in and through us to the glory of the Father. However, we must humble ourselves and first wash our minds with Biblical truth if we expect to attain the peace of God which surpasses all understanding (Phil. 4:7).

Application

1. When you think about peace in the life of your family, what does that realistically look like?
2. What is the peace of God which surpasses understanding?
3. Why is busyness so detrimental to peace and contentment?
4. What idols can you eliminate from your daily schedule to spend more quality time with God and those you love?
5. How does the lack of peace you are experiencing influence your spiritual health?
6. How can you promote peace in your home and community by being a peacemaker to others?
7. Why does inner peace protect you from reacting in anger?

Prayer

Lord, when I look around, I see a world in disarray and chaos. People appear so unhappy, discontent, and angry with one another. However, when I reflect upon my own heart, I see a similar war raging within me. I am agitated far too easily and create greater division than peace with my tongue. I see how busyness has caused more stress and anxiety than I ever realized. When I am on edge, it causes others to walk on eggshells around me. I hate that others are afraid of how I might react. Help me be a peacemaker who guards his tongue and prioritizes quality time with You, so I may walk in Your truth and experience peace which surpasses all understanding. I need to prioritize my time more wisely and that begins with rediscovering the joy of my salvation which is found in You. Amen.

Day 29 – Vengeance

> *"Beloved, never avenge yourselves but leave it to the wrath of God, for it is written, 'Vengeance is mine, I will repay, says the Lord.'"*
>
> — Romans 12:19 —

Hatred is like drinking poison and expecting someone else to die. It destroys within because it consumes the mind and tempts us to repay evil with evil. A man filled with hatred in his heart is a danger, not only to himself but others as well. For if ideal conditions and opportunity presents itself, he is likely to act out in unrighteous anger and yield to his emotions. Hatred is powerful. It can tempt us to react violently in ways we never thought possible and cause more destruction in its wake than we can imagine. Hatred should not be taken lightly, yet we often yield to pursuing vengeance and then wonder why we feel so fed up, discontent, and regretful of the consequences our actions elicited.

The far greater concern is that from Scripture's perspective, hatred cannot live in the heart of a Christ-follower. It wages war against the Holy Spirit living inside us. **"If anyone says, 'I love God,' and hates his brother, he is a liar; for he who does not love his brother whom he has seen cannot love God whom he has not seen" (1 John 4:20)**. Bottom-line, it does not matter how others may have mistreated us. If we call ourselves Christians, we represent the name of Jesus and must love and forgive others rather than hate those who have sinned against us. Drinking the poison of vengeance and yielding to hatred only magnifies our spiritual immaturity. It also calls into question the authenticity of our faith in Christ when we choose to hate rather than forgive.

Fatherly influence is one chapter in **"Wilderness Survival, Volume-1,"** which tends to stoke up the flames of wrath and vengeance in the hearts of men I have shepherded. The level of intensity and rage which pours out from those who were abused by their fathers or whose fathers failed to protect them from the abuse of others is catastrophic. When they share their stories, my heart breaks for the pain they have experienced but more so for the bitterness and resentment they carry to this day. What many fail to realize is withholding forgiveness does nothing to punish others. It only self-inflicts with wounds which will never heal or fade away until we learn to forgive and let go of our desire for vengeance.

Forgiving others is not easy. Until we walk a mile in someone else's shoes, we will never fully understand the depth and breadth of pain and suffering many people carry with them, nor the spiritual warfare which rages uncontrollably in their minds, bloodthirsty for justice. All we can do is trust God's Word which warns us to not harbor pain, bitterness, and resentment toward others. God wants us to be set free from the sin of vigilante justice, not enslaved by its desire. **"Let all bitterness and wrath and anger and clamor and slander be put away from you, along with all malice. Be kind to one another, tenderhearted, forgiving one another, as God in Christ forgave you"** (Ephesians 4:31-32).

Vengeance is a burden reserved for the Lord alone. When we attempt to take matters into our own hands, we stand in His holy place and assume we can weigh the scales of justice. How foolish! From God's perspective, we are just as guilty of sin as those who have sinned against us, because we have allowed Satan to poison our minds with hate. However, Jesus warns that retaliation does nothing to satisfy our fleshly desires. It only makes us liable to judgment as well. That is why we must love and forgive our enemies so we can stand before the Lord on judgment day with a clear conscience. **"For if you forgive others their sins, your heavenly Father will also forgive you, but if you do not forgive others their sins, neither will your Father forgive your sins" (Matthew 6:14-15)**.

I have witnessed the desire for vengeance rage through my wife's mind when I confessed my sexual immorality to her. The desire for revenge to give me a taste of my own medicine consumed her mind, for I had ripped her heart to shreds by my selfishness, dishonesty, and manipulation. All she felt was writhing pain in the deepest part of her soul, and vengeance stood at the doorway of her heart ready to take residence. However, by faith, she found the courage and strength to not react but respond in love. Her hope was in Christ and the wisdom of Biblical counseling to repair our marital covenant. Amber entrusted our marriage to the Lord and removed divorce from the table so that she was not tempted to take vengeance into her own hands.

The key to overcoming vengeance is by learning to forgive. It releases us from the responsibility of being judge, jury, and executioner for those who have grievously sinned against us. It also purges bitterness from our hearts and allows us to love our enemies rather than persecute them. Granted, it is not easy learning to forgive someone who denies wrongdoing, justifies sin, blame shifts responsibility, or could ultimately care less about how we feel. That is not our concern, though, for God wants us to love those who have hurt us and forgive because we have been forgiven. Only then will we be free from the chains of vengeance which tempt us daily.

Application

1. Why is taking personal vengeance so tempting?
2. What do you regret about vengeance you have taken against someone you love?
3. Why is forgiveness the key to overcoming vengeful desires?
4. How have you been on the receiving end of vengeance? What did you learn as a result?
5. How can you let go of bitterness and resentment and love your enemies instead?
6. What hinders you from playing judge, jury, and executioner when others have sinned against you?
7. How can the Gospel of salvation teach you to love your enemies and pray for those who persecute you?

Prayer

Lord, vengeance is a difficult topic for me to reconcile in my heart and mind. On one hand, I have sinned against You and deserve the wrath of Your judgment. However, I have also been sinned against by others and the temptation to avenge myself is intense. Help me focus my attention on the log in my eye before I try to remove the speck from the eye of those who have hurt me. I do not want to be consumed by the desire for vengeance. Rather, I want to lay those volatile and resentful emotions at the foot of Your cross where healing is found. Help me to let go of my bitterness and pain and show grace to others, because You have been merciful to me. Help me trust Your ability to judge others, not my own. Amen.

Day 30 – Mourning

> *"No one born of God makes a practice of sinning,*
> *for God's seed abides in him; and he cannot keep on sinning,*
> *because he has been born of God."*
>
> — 1 John 3:9 —

There is one instance in which we are allowed to hate and that concerns the worship of false idols in our hearts. We must channel our hatred toward personal sin because it separates us from God. Jesus taught in His sermon on the mount that we should mourn our sins (Matt. 5:4) and perform spiritual amputation, if needed, to ensure we are not being led astray by temptation (Matt. 18:8-9). In many ways, a man cannot be transformed by the Holy Spirit unless he loathes his sins. God leaves no margin for error because His Word specifically details which sins He hates, for they are an abomination to Him and invoke the fury of His wrathful judgment.

It may seem illogical, but to understand God's love, a man must immerse himself in the reality of God's impending wrath. They are equal and opposite aspects of His divine character. One cannot exist without the other because they explain each other's purpose. In other words, God's grace is so amazing because His wrath is so intense. Keep in mind, the Lord is not some giant teddy bear or genie in the sky whose desire is to grant all our wishes and ignore our sins. The only thing God the Father ever turned His face from was His own Son whom He crushed to set us free (Isa. 53:10). That is how much God hates sin—enough to sacrifice Jesus so we could escape the eternal fires of hell for our transgressions.

Movies such as the Passion of the Christ which graphically display the brutal flogging and disfiguration of Jesus are meant to grab our attention because we have become desensitized to sin. Violence is merely an example of what we see regularly on television, in movies, and in video game simulations. Yet when we allow conviction to connect the dots from our knowledge of what God's Word says to the reality of our hearts' depravity, the only response we should have is utter hatred and disgust for the idols we worship. At times, the Bible may feel like just a fictional story than a living entity (Heb. 4:12). However, we are extremely short-sighted if that is truly what we believe. No, we must hate and loathe our sins with a determined ferocity which promotes immediate change in our lives to free us from slavery and bondage.

I am extremely passionate about the validity of Scripture because we will never know how to mourn our sins until we admit we have a faith problem. For many years, I thought I trusted God but truly did not. I knew what Scripture said but chose to go my own way instead. What I learned is that my perspective of Scripture must transform in my heart from ink on a page to life-giving truth. It must for me to have any chance of defeating sin in my life. Therefore, when I find myself craving worldly pleasures and sin is crouching at my door, what I believe about God and His Word is the only thing that matters. For if I do not believe He will provide a way of escape from temptation and remind myself that He is my joy and salvation, I will yield to sin and crucify Christ who willingly died to set me free.

Every Christian man knows what it feels like to struggle with sin and stand before the door of pleasure, ready and willing to walk in without the slightest concern for its consequences. The desire we feel can be so intense that we cannot think of anything else, yet our conscience reminds us of what God says about yielding to temptation. That moment is as real as it gets because we must reconcile how much we truly hate our sins. If we do, then God's Word is living and active in us. However, if we do not, then we must admit we have allowed Scripture to become nothing more than ink on a page in our minds.

Freedom from the power of sin is an issue of faith, hope, and trust in God's sovereign provision of salvation. The sooner we realize it, the better off we will be resisting temptation. It is humbling when we realize that trust is our greatest failure, not the sins we battle daily. Perhaps that is why Jesus prescribed mourning as the repentant posture we must display to receive forgiveness of sins. Mourning demonstrates self-recognition—that we have not merely chosen poorly when we yield to our flesh but have fallen because we did not trust God's Word. Faith and trust are intertwined. Therefore, if we do not believe what God says, enough to follow His commands and turn away from sin, we have a massive trust problem which magnifies the weakness and immaturity of our faith.

If we have been exposed to the truth of God's Word, we cannot turn a blind eye to what it says. Rather, we are held liable to obey its commands because we have been exposed to the light of absolute truth. **"For if we go on sinning deliberately after receiving the knowledge of the truth, there no longer remains a sacrifice for sins, but a fearful expectation of judgment, and a fury of fire that will consume the adversaries" (Hebrews 10:26–27).** We simply cannot do as we please without reaping the consequences of our actions. That is why we will give account on judgment day, not merely for yielding to sin but for our lack of faith. In turn, that should compel us to weep and mourn bitterly because we recognize our depravity and that Jesus gave His life to set us free.

Application

1. When you consider hatred, what instantly comes to mind?
2. Why is it easier to hate others than mourn your own sins?
3. Why is hatred of sin critical to overcoming temptation?
4. What are the dangers of allowing temptation to fester in your heart and mind?
5. Read Proverbs 6:16-19. Which of the six things the Lord hates do you relate to most? How so?
6. How can unresolved sin destroy a man from within?
7. When you have truly mourned your sins, what level of joy and freedom have you experienced? How so?
8. Which sins do you need to mourn about today?

Prayer

Lord, when I look in the mirror, I often fail to see how prideful and self-righteous I have become. I think more highly of myself than I ought, which tempts me to minimize my sins rather than take full responsibility for the damages I cause. The more I reflect, the more I realize why sin and temptation continue to plague my heart and mind. I have lost touch with what it means to weep and mourn over my sins, because I am not taking time to see my soul's depravity from Your holy perspective. Help me avoid being spiritually blind to my own blindness but to see my sins through the conviction of Your Word. You died for my sins, Lord. I never want to take that precious gift for granted, but I am afraid I have far too often. Please break me of my pride and renew a right spirit within me. Amen.

Day 31 - Greed

> *"Woe to you, scribes and Pharisees, hypocrites!*
> *For you clean the outside of the cup and the plate, but inside*
> *they are full of greed and self-indulgence."*
>
> — *Matthew 23:25* —

How many of us would admit to being greedy? How many times in our lives have we disregarded the needs of others to ensure our personal desires were taken care of first? Greed is one of those ugly reflections in the mirror we prefer to ignore because there are no excuses for it. It bathes in the murky waters of selfishness and positions us above others, whether we realize it or not. Greed is the epitome of self-destruction because it is cancer to the soul. A man consumed by greediness has no excuse. Rather, he will give an account to the Lord on judgment day for the selfish attitude of his heart and his disdain for love and generosity.

The biggest problem with greed is it poisons our minds into believing everything we have in our personal possession belongs to us, not God. No longer are we faithful stewards of His abundant resources. Instead, greed convinces us that we are masters of our own domain because the fruits of our labor came solely by the sweat of our brow and work of our hands. God's sovereignty plays no part in the heart of a man who believes his financial fortune is the product of personal achievement. However, assuming we play any part in the blessings we enjoy and appreciate is utter nonsense. We are rich because God has given us the joy, honor, and opportunity to steward His resources, not because we are worthy in any way.

One of Jesus' parables speaks directly to the issue of greed. **"And he told them a parable, saying, 'The land of a rich man produced plentifully, and he thought to himself, "What shall I do, for I have nowhere to store my crops?" And he said, "I will do this: I will tear down my barns and build larger ones, and there I will store all my grain and my goods. And I will say to my soul, 'Soul, you have ample goods laid up for many years; relax, eat, drink, be merry.'" But God said to him, "Fool! This night your soul is required of you, and the things you have prepared, whose will they be?" So is the one who lays up treasure for himself and is not rich toward God'"** (Luke 12:16–21). The rich man pridefully assumed his wealth was earned rather than given by God and foolishly forgot that his riches were meant to share generously, not hoard selfishly.

The simple truth is the more material possessions we have, the harder it is to let go and share them with others. Due to our selfish sin nature, we always seem to protect our best interests, first and foremost. That is why we must intentionally shift our perspective from sole propriety to stewardship and asset management since all we have belongs to God. In other words, God owns it all and graciously allows us to manage what rightfully belongs to Him. That can be a tough pill to swallow for those who believe their success was achieved by the hard work and determination they personally invested. However, we cannot lose sight that our ability to live, breathe, and work are blessings which enable us to live and earn an income. Therefore, we cannot take them for granted.

The older I get, the more overwhelmed I am by all of the material possessions my family has acquired through the years. We have had to relocate due to my job four times and have continued to fill bigger houses with each move. Now that I am on the backend of my career, all I desire is to downsize our home and give away the majority of all we have accumulated. My perspective has basically shifted from personal enjoyment to generosity. For if I am not using something I own, someone else should have the opportunity to benefit from it instead.

It makes no sense for us to hoard more and more stuff when the abundance of our riches could be a blessing to others. Therefore, we are wise to clean house and evaluate our giving with open hands rather than clenched fists, especially as our children get older and leave the nest. We know God has blessed us far more than we can fathom, which is why we should earnestly desire to declutter and bless others as the Lord allows. We certainly wish we could go back in time and resist accumulating so much, but it also gives us ample opportunity to bless others as well. Therefore, we should be thankful to God for the chances to use what He's graciously given us to meet the practical needs of others.

Sometimes, it is hard not to be greedy. Whether we grew up rich or poor, the same selfish attitude can devour our minds and darken our hearts to the needs of others. Worry can wreak havoc on our psyche and tempt us to believe we need more to survive. If we grew up poor, we likely worry about finances and whether we will have enough money when times are tough. However, we must realize how blessed we are compared to the overwhelming majority of people worldwide and begin appreciating God's provision. If anything, having more tempts us to idolize money. That is why greed is so dangerous because it is never content. It craves more until we are fat, lazy, and indifferent to those less fortunate than ourselves, hoarding pleasures till the day we stand before the judgment seat of Christ and give account for our selfishness.

Application

1. What does greed look like in the heart of someone who grew up poor vs. someone who grew up with abundance?
2. What is the difference between contentment and greed?
3. Is there an exception to the rule where greed is allowed by God? How so?
4. How do you relate to the rich man's perspective in the parable of the rich fool (Luke 12:13-21)?
5. How have you been wounded by someone's greed? What did you learn from that experience?
6. What are the dangers of living coldhearted and indifferent to the needs of others?
7. How can you avoid falling victim to greed in your own life?

Prayer

Lord, whether my heart is consumed by greed, I know I can easily fall victim to worrying about whether my personal needs will be met. You have given me so much, yet I often look at my life from a glass-half-empty perspective. Help me count my blessings and not complain about what I lack. Teach me to give more of the talents and resources You have graciously provided so that I may be a blessing to others in Your name. I do not want to be known as a man who cared very little for generosity. Therefore, help me die to greed and put the needs of others before my selfish desires. No matter the cost, help me seek opportunities to sacrifice my time serving others as much as I give financially to help as well. Amen.

Day 32 – Generosity

"Give, and it will be given to you. Good measure, pressed down, shaken together, running over, will be put into your lap. For with the measure you use it will be measured back to you."

— Luke 6:38 —

Generosity is about living intentionally and opportunistically with open hands rather than clenched fists. It is therapy for the soul because it is a choice to return what rightfully belongs to God. It is also an act of paying forward what the Lord has graciously given us by wisely managing His resources to the best of our abilities. Generosity is immersed in the purified waters of thankfulness and gratitude for all Jesus Christ sacrificed for us on the cross of Calvary. Therefore, we should be compelled to look first to the interests of others and give generously without assumption or expectation, rather than sparingly, begrudgingly, or under obligation.

A man who is self-absorbed and unwilling to share God's blessings will ultimately realize on judgment day that hoarding the Lord's resources for himself was meaningless. In other words, he can selfishly collect everything God has given for his use only, but he will never experience the joy of generosity if he is always catering to his flesh before considering the needs of others. Greediness cuts us off from helping to solve the lack of resources in our community. Generosity opens the door and welcomes in those who are less fortunate and in dire straits, far more than we could ever fathom.

Generosity is not just exclusive to money. It includes our time and talent. For example, a man willing to enter a disaster-relief zone and rebuild homes because he has construction experience is an enormous blessing to those who have lost everything. Our talents could be in the area of compassion whereby we visit elderly in nursing homes who rarely receive visitors. Anything and everything God puts on our hearts to look outside our comfort zone and minister to others can be a unique opportunity to display the love of Jesus to lost souls. The key is identifying what resources God has provided us and then proactively utilizing those gifts to impact lives for the Gospel.

When I was born, I only had one out of four grandparents still living. My grandfather (born in 1904) began his family late and I was the last of five children as well, so there was a seventy-four-year age difference between the two of us. By the time I reached my final years of high-school, my grandfather (in his early 90's) had lost the ability to drive himself or mow his own lawn. So, every week I would go over to his house and cut the grass. On Sundays, I would pick him up and we would attend church together. Granted, that is not what most boys envision doing in their teenage years. However, those are some of the most precious memories I hold close to my heart today.

One of the things my grandfather always wanted to do when I visited was to eat together. If I cut the grass, we would go out after for a hamburger and fries. On Sundays, he would want us to get lunch after church at a family diner. He was never one to say much, but that was not the point. He valued quality time with loved ones as the greatest honor and privilege of his life, so just spending time together was everything to him. I never realized how sacrificing my time was as much a blessing to him as it was to me. However, I clearly see that lesson now and am thankful I had the opportunity to spend those years together before he passed away during my senior year of college.

Oftentimes, we think we need a healthy bank account to make a difference in this world, but that is a lie. God could care less how much money we possess because the attitude of our hearts is what concerns Him most. **"Each one must give as he has decided in his heart, not reluctantly or under compulsion, for God loves a cheerful giver" (2 Corinthians 9:7)**. That is why the Lord challenges us to test Him with our giving, because our faith can grow exponentially or remain stifled based on how generous we are with the gifts, talents, and resources He has provided. **"Bring the full tithe into the storehouse, that there may be food in my house. And thereby put me to the test, says the LORD of hosts, if I will not open the windows of heaven for you and pour down for you a blessing until there is no more need" (Malachi 3:10)**.

In the end, our spiritual health and maturity of faith can be measured by our willingness to share everything we have with others. Being generous is not something we do as Christians. It is part of our DNA. It is who we are as followers of Jesus Christ because our Lord and Savior gave all He had to save us. Therefore, we are without excuse if we withhold our tithes and remain self-absorbed, looking out for our own interests and disregarding the plight of others. Greed is cancerous to the soul, but generosity is the antidote which can cure us from the poison of selfishness. All we must do is to keep our eyes open and look for opportunities where we can invest our time, energy, and resources meeting the needs of others in Jesus' name and for His glory.

Application

1. What does it mean to give by paying-it-forward?
2. How often do you stop and count your blessings? What changes could you make to thank God more often?
3. Why is generosity a pillar of the Christian faith?
4. What hinders you from being generous with your time, energy, and resources?
5. Who benefits most when you take time to generously bless others? How so?
6. Why is tithing an issue of the heart and not the wallet?
7. How has God blessed you when you have sacrificially given your tithe back to Him with joy in your heart?

Prayer

Lord, thank You for dying on the cross for my sins. I know that I do not spend enough time thanking You for all the abundant blessings You provide. I can do nothing apart from Your sovereign grace in my life, yet I lose sight of what You call me to do in loving and serving others. Please help me to stop acting as if all I financially possess is mine but to give the shirt off my back to anyone in need. It is my honor to share with others all that I have. Please convict me to do more with the gifts, talents, and resources in my possession. Help me live with open hands, willing and able to serve You without hesitation. I long to expect nothing in return. Therefore, give me eyes to see and ears to hear how I can be of service to others according to the Spirit's conviction. Amen.

Day 33 - Deviation

"Let no one say when he is tempted, 'I am being tempted by God,' for God cannot be tempted with evil, and he himself tempts no one."

— James 1:13 —

When Adam and Eve ate the forbidden fruit in the Garden of Eden, sin entered the world and changed the course of history. However, along with it came accusations, blame-shifting, and denial as they were confronted by God with the enormity of their decision. They began pointing the finger instead of owning their choices and accepting full responsibility for their actions. **"The man said, 'The woman whom you gave to be with me, she gave me fruit of the tree, and I ate.' Then the LORD God said to the woman, 'What is this that you have done?' The woman said, 'The serpent deceived me, and I ate'"** (Genesis 3:12–13).

Covering up their sin ultimately proved detrimental because the Lord banished them from the garden, for they deviated from the stern warning and wisdom of His Word. Similarly, we often think we know better than God and blaze our own trail due to arrogance. Pride rears its ugly head and we assume there is an alternate route to peace and contentment which the Lord is withholding from us. Therefore, we hedge our bet, plunge into uncharted waters, and then cry out for God to save us when things do not turn out the way we planned.

However, the more we journey off-trail, the more confused and disoriented we become. Far too many people have lost their lives in the rugged wilderness by not sticking to the trail and remaining on course. They assumed there was a logical shortcut, so they took a chance and accepted the risk, not realizing how catastrophic their decision would prove to be. In hindsight, the same logic applies spiritually. God has given us everything we need to survive the trials and dangers of this world. However, we are often too hardhearted to yield to His sovereignty and too stubborn to admit we are grossly ill-equipped to handle the storms which lie ahead.

That is why deviation is one of the most subtle sins we face, for even the slightest miscalculation can prove catastrophic and ultimately determine whether we live or die. Well-intentioned Christians throughout the ages have found themselves lost in the wilderness of spiritual warfare because they allowed a seed of arrogance to take root in their hearts. Why? Because when a tree of self-reliance grows, it shades us from the light of God's truth and hinders us from separating fact from fiction. In other words, we cannot recognize or identify a counterfeit because we have never studied the original.

When I open my Bible and begin reading passages such as 1 Peter 3:7 which says, **"Husbands, live with your wives in an understanding way, showing honor to the woman as the weaker vessel,"** I am convicted. I fail miserably at obeying God's command. For example, when Amber and I talk, my ability to discredit her opinion or ignore her accountability proves how guilty I am for doing the complete opposite of what Scripture teaches. I am not showing her honor when I cut her off mid-sentence and interrupt her train of thought. Instead, I have chosen poorly and deviated from what I should be doing as a sensitive, caring, and understanding husband who honors his wife.

For many years, this was an area of weakness until I realized how my interruptions, corrections, and assumptions were plaguing our marriage. Amber did not feel loved because I was more focused on getting my point across than hearing what she had to say. She also did not feel valued because I acted as if my opinions were more important. She felt steamrolled by my pride and arrogance, and I was too naïve to comprehend how much damage I was inflicting because I had deviated from the wisdom of God's Word. In other words, I did things my own way and how I felt comfortable, regardless of how she felt.

Even the slightest deviation in judgment can prove tragic. The Bible is full of examples of people who suffered greatly for what we would consider minor errors in judgment. Lot's wife looked back to see Sodom burn and turned into a pillar of salt; Uzzah touched the ark of the covenant to keep it from falling and died unexpectedly; Ananias and Sapphira sold a plot of land but lied about the details of the transaction and perished. Therefore, anytime we choose to silence the Spirit of God who leads and guides us, we run the risk of sinning by going our separate way and ignoring the teachings of Holy Scripture.

God's Word is not a nice-to-have but a need-to-have in our lives. For without truth to light our way unto righteousness, we will base our decisions on personal experiences and opinions rather than Scripture. In the end, deviating from the protection of God's Word is not merely risky but foolish. It magnifies how prideful we are to think we know more than the almighty Creator of the universe. Unfortunately, we fail the Lord when we lean on our own understanding. Therefore, we must acknowledge our foolishness, repent of our sins, and stop our continual deviation from God's Word to avoid impending judgment.

Application

1. What does it mean to deviate from God's Word?
2. When are you prone to lean on your own understanding rather than look to the Lord for wisdom and discernment?
3. How have you suffered from taking shortcuts when you should have stuck to the plan? What did you learn?
4. Are you more prone to accept the consequences of your actions or blame shift and accuse others instead?
5. Give a practical example of a Biblical teaching you are not living up to. How can you begin making changes moving forward to apply what Scripture teaches?
6. Is God's Word a nice-to-have or a need-to-have in your life? Do your actions say otherwise? Why or why not?

Prayer

Lord, more often than not, I lean on my own understanding rather than yield to Your wisdom. Why I continue to do things my own way makes no sense, yet I continue to fall right back into sin and make poor choices time and again. How can I be so arrogant to think I know better? It is becoming glaringly obvious that Your Word is not written on my heart as much as it should. Otherwise, I would not forget to heed Your wisdom so often. Please help me die to selfishness and temptation so I can live for holiness and honor You. Your Word clearly teaches what is right and wrong. Convict me to stop thinking that I always know better. I have deviated from righteousness for far too long. I repent of my wickedness, Lord. Please forgive me and make me whole again. Amen.

Day 34 – Accountability

> *"Why do you pass judgment on your brother? Or you, why do you despise your brother? For we will all stand before the judgment seat of God; for it is written, 'As I live, says the Lord, every knee shall bow to me, and every tongue shall confess to God.' So then each of us will give an account of himself to God."*
>
> — *Romans 14:10–12* —

Accountability is a spiritual discipline that everyone needs yet few actually have in their lives. It is where the rubber meets the road for a Christ-follower, for no man who desires to live a Godly life can reach his full potential without a trusted friend calling out his sins and holding him accountable to the truth of Scripture. Having Godly and trusted Christ-followers call out the blind spots in our moral character is paramount to success. We need the body of Christ to expose the sins we are committing and the temptations we allow to fester at the door of our hearts. Otherwise, we are likely to wander from God's truth and suffer the consequences of our actions.

It is not easy allowing others full access to our lives, but it is critical for spiritual health. Scripture reminds us, **"Two are better than one, because they have a good reward for their toil. For if they fall, one will lift up his fellow. But woe to him who is alone when he falls and has not another to lift him up!" (Ecclesiastes 4:9–10)**. Therefore, we must trust those who adhere to Scripture to ask us hard questions and guide us towards the wisdom of God's Word rather than human understanding. That is one easy way to identify who should hold us accountable. For if those we trust do not believe the Word of God, cover-to-cover, then we should question their discernment if they cannot Biblically defend their advice.

No one holds me more accountable than Amber because she is the most Godly person I know, and her wisdom is always bathed in Scripture. She is also great at accountability and sees my justification, blame-shifting, and minimization of sins a mile away. She pulls no punches and holds me accountable to a zero-tolerance standard. I would not be the man I am today without her willingness to speak truth in love and overcome my defensive posture. However, as hard as it is to hear what she has to say, I know her heart is always pure because her intent is to protect me from spiritual warfare. That is why she continues to speak truth, because she knows I need to hear it to become a more Godly man, husband, and father.

The problem with accountability is we fail to appreciate the wounds our family and friends are willing to endure when we reject their discernment and attack them in return. It takes an incredible amount of humility to listen and apply the wisdom of those who point us to Scripture rather than tell us what we want to hear. **"Faithful are the wounds of a friend; profuse are the kisses of an enemy" (Proverbs 27:6).** That is also how we can discern who truly cares about our spiritual well-being—when they tell us what we need to hear rather than what we want to hear. They are willing to risk the relationship rather than dishonor the Lord's teachings.

Recently, Amber and I had the opportunity to discuss why I struggle with prayer. Like most men, I often feel intimidated praying with her, so I avoid it altogether rather than fix the problem. I tried playing the "I did not grow up with a good example" card, but she was not buying it. I even blamed her for mothering me too much, but she rejected that excuse as well and gave me a piece of her mind for insinuating she was the problem! Finally, there was nothing I could do but own my sins and accept that I had been failing our family as spiritual leader. There was no one to blame but myself, and her willingness to hold me accountable urged me to make positive changes which have greatly benefitted our marriage ever since.

For decades, my lackadaisical approach to prayer has been a sore spot in our home. In Amber's eyes, nothing else matters to our health than growing together spiritually. Prayer and devotions are things she has talked about countless times, yet I have been slow to change. Granted, she could have thrown in the towel and gave up hope because I repeatedly failed to make good on my promises to pray more, but she has persevered despite my laziness and continued to point me to God's Word. I am certainly not a perfect man by any means, and I still struggle to implement certain spiritual disciplines into my life. However, I am determined to change because of my wife's selfless love and her Biblical accountability.

We all need assistance in life, but we often resist asking for directions, if we can help it, because our pride gets in the way. However, who cares whether we are embarrassed to admit our faults? If we truly desire to be more Godly men, we must get honest with ourselves and those we love. Otherwise, we will continue living in the darkness of sins with no hope for a brighter tomorrow. Therefore, accountability must be a discipline we prioritize daily to display the attributes of a Godly man. For without it, we are nothing more than hypocrites acting as if we have it together when nothing could be further from the truth.

Application

1. What are the benefits of having accountability in your life?
2. How do you hold yourself accountable to God's Word?
3. How are you unwilling to be held accountable? Why?
4. What do you believe accountability should practically look like to be effective?
5. How have you struggled in your faith journey due to a lack of Biblical accountability?
6. How have you gained wisdom from the wounds of a friend when he or she has spoken truth in love to you?
7. Are you open or closed off to accountability from your immediate family? Why?
8. How have the wounds of a friend saved your life and grown your faith in Christ?

Prayer

Lord, I know I am held accountable by the power of Your Word, yet I struggle prioritizing relationships which guard my heart and mind. I tend to lean on my own understanding far more than I should and my sins reflect my lack of discipline in this area. I need the body of Christ to hold me accountable which inevitably begins at home. Help me embrace truth when my loved ones bring things to my attention so I can make positive changes that glorify You. Help me also die to pride and allow loved ones access to my heart and soul. I cannot do this alone, otherwise I will fall again into sin. Therefore, give me ears to hear the Spirit's conviction. Amen.

Day 35 – Worry

"Peace I leave with you; my peace I give to you. Not as the world gives do I give to you. Let not your hearts be troubled, neither let them be afraid."

— John 14:27 —

We all worry, but to what degree does it monopolize our time and attention? We often worry about the trials today might bring and brace ourselves for what we assume will go wrong. As parents, we worry about our children's health and safety at school when we are not present. As children, we sometimes worry whether we are truly loved, supported, and accepted by our parents. There are plenty of things to consume our minds on a daily basis. However, when will we cast our cares upon the Lord and stop bearing the weight of stress and anxiety ourselves? What good is it to worry about the future when it is unknown and uncontrollable?

One of Jesus' most famous teachings centered on anxiety. **"And which of you by being anxious can add a single hour to his span of life?" (Matthew 6:27)**. His message was simple. Worry can become a false idol we worship if our hearts are not focused on our Father in heaven. Keep in mind, before Jesus addressed the topic of anxiety, He warned His audience to avoid the pleasures of this world and lay up their treasures in heaven instead. **"For where your treasure is, there your heart will be also" (Matthew 6:21)**. For if our faith and hope are dependent upon the empty promises of this world, we will be enslaved to anxiety which cripples our minds with fear, doubt, stress, and worry.

As a father of four daughters, I am always concerned about safety. There is nothing I have prayed about more over the past 18-years, because we live in a dangerous world. Today, human trafficking is a real concern which requires me to always be on guard to ensure my girls are protected. When they were little and we would go shopping, I made sure they were directly by my side. If they were even a few steps behind, I told them to immediately get to where I could see them so I knew their exact location. It was not that I did not trust them. Rather, I did not trust everyone else, and that skepticism fueled my over-protective tendencies to punish anyone who dared harm them.

As they grew older, my anxiety only increased because they were going places with friends and driving themselves. I had to trust that they would be safe and secure without me there to guard them, which was excruciatingly difficult considering how over-protective I am with my family. However, God has taught me a hard lesson as a father which has been a tough pill to swallow. Namely, while my job as a "girl dad" is to serve and protect my daughters to the best of my ability, they were His before they were mine and He can protect them far better than I ever could.

It can be difficult to let go of anxiety when we feel it is justified or warranted. For example, worrying about personal health or safety is a fair concern. However, it should never consume our minds where we lose sight of who is ultimately in control. We serve the sovereign Creator of the universe who is all-knowing, all-powerful, and eternal. There is not a situation in which we will find ourselves where God is not in complete control. He always has our best interest in mind. Therefore, to question His sovereignty would be ridiculous considering He spoke the entire world into existence.

Undoubtedly, King David faced the same type of anxiety we do. However, He knew that as long as his faith never failed, no one could harm him. **"The LORD is my light and my salvation; whom shall I fear? The LORD is the stronghold of my life; of whom shall I be afraid? When evildoers assail me to eat up my flesh, my adversaries, and foes, it is they who stumble and fall. Though an army encamp against me, my heart shall not fear; though war arise against me, yet I will be confident" (Psalm 27:1–3)**. David had plenty to be anxious about, yet he found the courage to drown out his anxiety and trust the Lord. Likewise, we are called to lean upon God when our future is unknown.

In many ways, worry is a defensive mechanism which signals that our faith in Christ is weak or lacking. Think of it like the dashboard gauges on a car, warning us that something is wrong. In other words, we need to pay close attention to remedy the problem if want to put an end to our worries. Granted, we may not want to admit that our failures boil down to a matter of faith, but how could Jesus be more clear in His sermon on the mount? Our Savior stands before us with the same message He delivered to the thousands who heard His sermon that day. Namely, that our heavenly Father loves us and will meet our needs, both temporary and eternal.

Therefore, we should have nothing to worry about. Our Savior conquered sin and death on the cross of Calvary and we have been set free from the bondage of anxieties of this world. **"Come to me, all who labor and are heavy laden, and I will give you rest. Take my yoke upon you, and learn from me, for I am gentle and lowly in heart, and you will find rest for your souls." (Matthew 11:28-29)**. For in Christ alone we find rest, and that is enough assurance to cast our cares upon Him rather than carrying them upon our shoulders like an eight-hundred-pound gorilla.

Application

1. Would others label you as anxious? Why or why not?
2. Which things consume your mind with unnecessary worry?
3. Do you believe it is sinful to worry? Why or why not?
4. How has anxiety caused sickness or physical ailments in your life? How have you chosen to self-medicate your problems rather than lean on God?
5. Why it so easy to shoulder the burden of anxiety yourself when Scripture encourages you to cast your cares upon the Lord instead?
6. Why is prayer critical to overcoming temptations to worry?
7. What are the dangers of allowing unresolved anxiety and worry to wage war in your heart and mind?

Prayer

Lord, You are Alpha and Omega, the beginning, and the end. Please forgive me for not acknowledging Your supreme authority more often. I am so overcome by anxiety at times that I forget You are sovereignly in control, working all things together for my good. Help me cast my cares upon You rather than foolishly attempting to overcome the schemes of the devil in my own strength. Only You have the power to defeat the enemy and I need to trust Your power rather than my own. I release my worries to You, knowing that nothing this side of heaven will steal my joy as long as I continue to lean upon You and not rely on myself. Thank you for being my ultimate way of escape. Your grace is truly amazing. Amen.

Day 36 - Patience

"The Lord is not slow to fulfill his promise as some count slowness, but is patient toward you, not wishing that any should perish, but that all should reach repentance."

— 2 Peter 3:9 —

We have likely heard the saying, "Do not pray for patience!" because heaven forbid, we welcome pain and hardship into our lives and be better off for it. What is unfortunate about our perspective of patience is that we assume the Lord has to cast down fire and brimstone from heaven and push us to the brink of insanity to gain perseverance. We act as if learning patience is punishment— a curse for those foolish enough to pray for opportunities to grow their faith. Unfortunately, that is not how God teaches us the hard lessons we need to grow spiritually. For if we truly desire to mature in our knowledge and understanding of patience, we must change our poor attitude and shift our perspective, seeking after it rather than avoiding it.

Patience is a lesson we learn in the moment and look back on at a later date from a vantage point of thanksgiving to God. It is never easy being expected to wait, especially when the trials we are facing are hyper-critical and difficult to bear, but God's timing is always perfect. We need not worry what tomorrow might bring because He holds the spectrum of time in the palm of His hands. Therefore, when trials come knocking at our door, the way we consider them with joy is by remembering that God is with us in the fire. All He expects in return is our complete surrender to His authority, obedience to His Word, and submission to His sovereign will.

When I had my heart attack, I actually had two separate stent surgeries. Both surgeries were identical, except in the first, they decided not to place a stent in my heart. Apparently, it was in a more difficult location than they felt comfortable operating. Also, the equipment needed was not available at that particular hospital, so a transfer was required. I was frustrated at first but understood why they held off after the fact. However, I was not expecting it would take a full day and a half to get transported from one facility to another. I just sat in my bed watching the clock turn, wondering when my heart would get fixed so I could go home. Whether I liked it or not, I had to wait patiently, and I hated sitting around with nothing but my thoughts to consume me.

Looking back, I am glad I had my heart procedure where I did. The surgeon did a great job and I have enjoyed having him as my cardiologist ever since. I did not understand why I had to spend five days between two hospitals to rectify my issues, but my stent was placed in the best heart hospital in the city by one of the best surgeons as well. I could not be upset with the outcome, no matter how long it took. I just remember sitting frustrated in my hospital bed having to wait for my second surgery. However, I could have also died had I not gotten to a hospital altogether, which is sobering to consider. In retrospect, having to wait was insignificant compared to what could have happened had I passed away at home.

Patience is always one of those hindsight blessings where we require distance from the heat of the moment to recognize and appreciate the silver-lining of God's grace at work. However, that is the essence of faith. We do not have all the answers and cannot predict the future, yet we are expected to trust the omniscient God of the universe who is Lord over all. That does not mean trust is easy. In the moment, it is difficult for us to see the forest through the trees. However, when we reach the mountaintop and look back on the journey of faith we traveled to learn patience, we appreciate the blood, sweat, and tears we invested to reach our summit.

Patience is truly an endurance test which does not come easily. We must train our minds to resist the flaming arrows of the enemy which tempt us to doubt God's sovereignty. Satan wants nothing more than to watch us throw in the towel and give up trusting God. That is why he ramps up his efforts and increases his spiritual warfare intensity the minute we lean into God's grace and commit to growing deeper roots of faith in Scripture. Satan knows that if he can tempt us to question God's sovereignty amid our trials, we will grow tired and impatient with our lack of reprieve and ultimately blame the Lord for our pain and struggles. In other words, Satan wants us to embolden our minds into believing that God is our primary enemy, not him.

However, when we filter our emotions and sift fact from fiction, it is easier to make wise decisions concerning how to handle the seasons of trials we find ourselves. Trials are meant to sanctify our faith and embolden our need and dependance on the Lord and His Word. We were never meant to solve our problems independently, which is why God's strength is required to endure trials. Undoubtedly, we do not have the ability to fight our own battles. We need the Holy Spirit. For when we trust the Spirit of God who dwells in our hearts, Satan must retreat, because Jesus defeated sin and death at Calvary. Therefore, when we are tempted to doubt God's timing, we can rest assured that He will meet our needs as He sees fit and in His perfect timing.

Application

1. How would you describe what a patient man looks like?
2. Have you ever prayed for patience? Why or why not?
3. What is the root cause of your impatience?
4. What compels you to distrust God's sovereignty amid trials and lean on your own understanding instead?
5. Why is patience a fruit of the Spirit? What does that mean?
6. How has God taught you the gift of patience recently?
7. How has a lack of Godly patience plagued your relationships with those who get on your nerves?
8. Why is patience a good test of spiritual maturity? What does it testify about your journey of faith?

Prayer

Lord, many times I have prayed that You would give me patience, not realizing in the moment what that truly meant. You intend for trials to test every fabric of my being, so that I relinquish control and learn to trust You rather than my personal strength or abilities. I know I am stubborn and refuse to lean upon Your Word the way I should. Help me surrender my pride and let You take the wheel so I may receive the fruit of patience in my life. I want to have self-control over my thoughts and feelings and not react when I should respond in faith. You are the sovereign Lord in whom I trust, but my faith often grows weary when pain and suffering are constant. Therefore, help me overcome my fears and trust in You when I feel like the walls are closing in. Amen.

Day 37 – Despair

> *"When the righteous cry for help, the Lord hears and delivers them out of all their troubles. The Lord is near to the brokenhearted and saves the crushed in spirit. Many are the afflictions of the righteous, but the Lord delivers him out of them all."*
>
> — Psalm 34:17-19 —

It is one thing to wonder if our personal trials will ever end. It is another to lose all faith, hope, and trust that God can do anything about it. Despair is an issue we all face, but do we consider hopelessness a sin? That seems pretty harsh, doesn't it? How about mourning the loss of a loved one or battling seasons of depression? What if a grievous crime is committed which damages our psyche? Is despair disallowed by God in the grieving process? There are many "what if" scenarios we can think of to rationalize our justification for despair. However, that does not mean we are sinning, or does it?

We must remember that despair and unbelief go hand-in-hand. We cannot read Scripture, place eternal faith in Christ, and then give up hope that He has the power to save us in our misery. Jesus defeated the powers of hell once and for all. How then is He suddenly incapable to help us through our seasons of pain and suffering? The truth is He is plenty capable. We simply do not want to trust His sovereign will because we demand that He save us according to our way and timing. Like a genie in a bottle, we expect

Him to grant our wishes. If he fails, then we have all the more reason to wallow in despair and give up hope, or so we think.

We often confuse grief with despair, but that is inaccurate. Despair says, "God, you are powerless to do anything about my problems. You do not care about me. If you did, you would do something!" Yet when we step back and filter our emotions out of the equation, what we are left with is hopelessness and unbelief. Keep in mind, unbelief in the power and sovereignty of God reveals a dependency on tangible evidence to justify our faith. We want physical proof that God is real and He hears us, but what He expects in return is unwavering faith and trust in His Son who died for our sins. **"Thomas answered him, 'My Lord and my God!' Jesus said to him, 'Have you believed because you have seen me? Blessed are those who have not seen and yet have believed'"** (John 20:28-29).

If our judgment is clouded with despair, we will never stop and listen for the voice of God speaking to us. Hopelessness drowns out our ability to not only see God at work all around us but to discern the wisdom of His Word. We cannot hear the Holy Spirit calling out when we are more concerned with complaining than listening. In other words, we are too busy talking to hear what God has to say. That is why despair is so dangerous, because we believe we are justified to hold our ground until God proves Himself. Only then will we believe! However, the more we hold fast to our foolish ways of thinking, the more we heap impending judgment upon our souls for sinning against the Lord due to unbelief.

There are friends and extended family members in my life whom I have despaired over because of their unwillingness to place saving faith in Christ. In some cases, I have lost hope that God can change the hardness of their hearts because I fail to pray about it. My lack of care and concern has become a root of bitterness and despair (which is sobering to admit) and an area where I have sinned against God. I now realize I have doubted His ability to break the pride of my loved ones and save them from self-destruction, because I have yet to see it happen. I am foolishly demanding proof and physical evidence of heart transformation instead of believing it can happen before I see it come to fruition.

When we pull back the mask of justification for our despair, we will likely see how susceptible we have become to hopelessness. Anytime we doubt God can do something, simply because He has not thus far, does not mean He is incapable. Rather, it means we must submit to His timing and not our own. God does not bow to the idol of our personal expectations. Rather, He pours out His wrath on Christ for our despair when we should receive the just penalty for our hopelessness and unbelief. How foolish are we to believe the Creator of the universe exists to do our bidding? Rather, we should echo the words of John the Baptist who solemnly declared concerning Jesus, **"He must increase, but I must decrease" (John 3:30)**.

The Lord allows us to freely grieve and mourn, but those seasons of life are not necessarily grounded in despair. For example, we can weep over the passing of a loved one and not lose hope in Christ. If anything, hope is the reason we lift our heads despite pain and suffering and count our trials as joy because of our faith in Jesus. Realistically, despair does not benefit our souls whatsoever. It merely enslaves our hearts into thinking God is absent and does not care about the difficulties we face. However, nothing could be further from the truth than assuming God is too busy for us. He loves us far more than we will ever know and protects us from dangers we cannot clearly see.

Application

1. How have you experienced despair in your life? How does it typically manifest itself?
2. Why is despair often mistaken as grieving and mourning? What should you grieve and mourn instead?
3. Do you consider despair a sin? Why or why not?
4. Is there any reason to lose hope in God? Why or why not?
5. How have you seen despair negatively impact those who are struggling to understand the meaning behind trials?
6. What does it mean to hope in Christ? Why does it matter?
7. How has Satan used despair to draw you away from the body of Christ to isolate your mind?

Prayer

Lord, thank You for the gift of Jesus who paid my eternal debt and set me free from the bondage of despair. I confess that I do not always appreciate the enormous sacrifice You made crushing Your Son with the weight of my guilt and shame. I tend to live tunnel-visioned on things which only impact me and allow my mind to dwell on hopelessness. I have nothing to be depressed about because what I struggle with pales in comparison to what others are facing. Please forgive my foolishness and help me see the blessings of trials in my life. Bind the enemy from baiting me into despair so I do not sin against You. You are gracious beyond measure, Lord. Help me never forget how patient You are with me, but to trust You when I cannot see the other side of the horizon. Amen.

Day 38 – Brokenness

> *"The sacrifices of God are a broken spirit; a broken and contrite heart, O God, you will not despise."*
>
> — Psalm 51:17 —

In order for transformational change to occur in our sinful hearts, we must come to the point where we are sick and tired of being sick and tired. In other words, we must hit rock bottom and experience brokenness to the point where we are not merely sorry for our sins but grieve them instead. **"Blessed are those who mourn, for they shall be comforted" (Matthew 5:4)**. Brokenness is the key which unlocks the door of eternal redemption, but we must recognize our sins as God sees them. Otherwise, we will suffer the fateful consequences of attempting to put a band-aid on a mortal wound. For we will die as a result, unaware of what we truly needed to survive.

It is pointless focusing on behavioral modifications when surgery is required deep within our hearts. That is why King David wrote Psalm 51 to demonstrate what repentance looks like from God's perspective. However, what we often gloss over is that David did not say the sacrifices of God are a broken heart. He did not highlight the need for a cleansed mind either. Instead, he said that God is ultimately concerned with a broken spirit, which reveals how we must posture our hearts before Him when we look in the mirror and see our sins from His righteous lens. In other words, ownership must accompany brokenness for us to be genuinely repentant.

Being broken in spirit constitutes surrender in the deepest parts of our being. It means we finally realize that we cannot save ourselves, so we turn our eyes toward heaven and relinquish control to Christ. A man who is spiritually broken could not be in a better position, because he has nowhere to go but up if he desires to become a Godly man, husband, and father. The challenge is our enemy knows how to push our buttons and tempt us to trade our faith in Christ for hopelessness. Satan knows if he can get us to believe our sins are too big, or that we are unworthy of forgiveness, we will succumb to despair and never taste victory.

Regrettably, at specific points in my life, I have contemplated what it would look like if I ended it all. I believe Satan promotes suicide as a simple and easy way to escape the trials of life, and that opportunity has crossed my mind on more than one occasion. I would like to say I have never wrestled with the thought. However, when emotions run high, it is tempting to take matters into my own hands and end the pain and suffering once and for all. For instance, while I was an extrovert growing up, I always used humor to deflect the pain I was harboring deep inside. Whether it was due to loneliness, isolation, or sin, putting up a front of being happy all the time was critical to deflect attention away from how I was truly feeling on the inside.

Thankfully, I never seriously sought an avenue to pursue suicide, but I have wondered whether my absence would be beneficial to others. Since that time, I have learned to manage my emotions through the truth of God's Word. Yet from time to time, those thoughts creep back into my mind in an attempt to overwhelm my soul. Case in point, after failing as a husband due to sexual sin, there have been moments of conflict between Amber and I that the enemy has dangled suicide before me as an escape from guilt, shame, and regret. He wants me to embrace the scarlet letter and accept that I never changed for the better. However, that is a lie, and I must remind myself daily of who I am in Christ to avoid falling into despair to the point of no return.

Brokenness is one of the most difficult positions we find ourselves, because we are completely vulnerable and fully exposed to the enemy's attack when we own our sins and step into the light. In that moment, pride is stripped away and we have nothing to cover our guilt, shame, and regret with other than the atoning blood of Jesus to redeem our sins. Truly, those are the most honest moments in our lives because we have no excuses. All we have are broken spirits willing to hear the truth of God's Word and believe what it says, perhaps for the first time in our lives. In many ways, that is what true repentance looks like. Therefore, we are wise to not allow Satan ample opportunity to attack our minds by seeking salvation in any form outside of faith in Jesus Christ.

Granted, there are certainly methods to self-medicate our problems and drown our sorrows in worldly pleasures, but that will only enslave us further. What we need is brokenness and a willingness for the Spirit of God to convict our hearts and draw us closer to Christ. For He stands fully resurrected at the foot of the cross to prove that we too can be free from the chains of emotional and psychological bondage, so long as we trade our sorrows for joy and take His yoke upon us. In return, He will bear our burdens and absorb the wrath of God for the forgiveness of our sins, but we must let go of our pride and relinquish control of our lives to Him. Only then will we drink from the cup of victory over sin and death, not because we deserve it, but because He loved us enough to die in our place.

Application

1. Why is brokenness a foundational pillar of repentance?
2. What sins in your life are you most broken about? Which still need to be broken by God?
3. How can you prevent brokenness from becoming despair?
4. How can you embrace the Spirit's conviction as a catalyst for change and transformation in your life?
5. Why is it important to be "sick and tired of being sick and tired" to overcome habitual sins in your life?
6. How has God redeemed you when you have sacrificed your broken spirit to Him?
7. What miracles has God performed in your heart when you have embraced brokenness and repented of your sins?

Prayer

Lord, for far too long I have been reluctant to completely surrender my pride and embrace brokenness for my sins. It seems I try everything short of obeying Your Word to dig myself out of the holes I have created, only to plunge deeper into thoughts of despair and hopelessness. Help me to never lose sight of the cross when my mind is overwhelmed with doubt and regret. Remind me of who I am in Christ so that I find lasting peace for my tired and weary soul. The enemy wants me to throw in the towel and accept defeat, but I know you have a plan and purpose for my life. Therefore, help me trust Your sovereign will and never lose hope in the joy of my salvation. I surrender all that I am to You, Lord. Amen.

Day 39 – Indifference

> *"I know your works: you are neither cold nor hot.*
> *Would that you were either cold or hot! So, because you are*
> *lukewarm, and neither hot nor cold,*
> *I will spit you out of my mouth."*
>
> — Revelation 3:15-16 —

What does it say about us if we know the right thing to do yet choose to ignore it and go our own way instead? How can we be the righteous men, husbands, and fathers God expects if we are lukewarm about sin and indifferent to His sovereign will? Truly, we are called to a far greater purpose than we realize, and it is time we wake up and embrace the role God designed for us in the Garden of Eden. God expects us to love, serve, and protect those within our care. That is why indifference must be a negative attribute we reject wholeheartedly. For the world needs men of righteous, moral character to lead the next generation, not ones who deflect their shepherding responsibility.

When we fail to take Scripture seriously, we communicate to others that absolute truth is inconsequential. If it were, we would rely solely on the Lord's wisdom and be ready to step onto the battlefield of spiritual warfare, properly armed with the sword of the Spirit by our side (Eph. 6:17). However, the dust collecting on our Bibles paints a far different picture and testifies to our lack of spiritual discipline and indifference to the power of Scripture. In other words, we may proclaim we believe God, but our personal behavior stands in stark contrast to the fact that we often view the absolute truth of His Word as ink on a page rather than life-giving wisdom.

Truly, we bear little fruit of the Spirit because we are cold and indifferent to righteousness. We view it as a nice-to-have rather than a need-to-have, pushing it to the bottom of our priority list in favor of sports, hobbies, and other comforts. We simply do not care about pleasing God as much as generations of old, yet we wonder why we are so tired and empty, devoid of purpose and indifferent to the cares and concerns of those around us. If only we would open our eyes and see that the fields are white for harvest (John 4:35), perhaps we would shift our thoughts and prioritize things which matter most, rather than worldly distractions which monopolize our time and attention.

Like most guys, I love sports. I grew up a huge fan of college football on Saturdays and pro football on Sundays. There was a time when I planned my schedule around watching games. However, when Amber and I got married, my priorities changed. Suddenly, I had to share the remote and balance my love of sports for things which I did not enjoy as much. She was okay with it at first but quickly grew tired of my desire to watch football all day long. When we started having kids, my schedule became even more demanding, which forced me to choose how I spent my time. I had to decide where my treasure truly belonged. That was difficult for me to accept at the time because watching sports was my temporary escape from the demands of reality.

It took a while, but I learned to die to selfish pleasures. I began to open my eyes to the opportunities God provided to prioritize my faith and family. I still enjoyed football, but I only watched a game when it did not interfere with family time. In the moment, it felt like a huge sacrifice. In retrospect, I cannot believe how foolish I was to place a meaningless idol above my family. I have since realized that playing a game with my little girls or having a faith conversation with my older teens is far more precious to me. Granted, I still watch a game from time to time and I passionately support my favorite teams, but it is rare to find me watching anything on television because it does not mean that much to me anymore.

When we read through Scripture, we quickly realize that grey does not exist in God's color palette regarding sin. He is either black or white, and He will judge our thoughts and actions regardless of whether we repent or not. Therefore, we must seriously consider whether we hold the same standard of righteousness that He does when we look in the mirror and self-examine our hearts. It simply comes down to whether we care enough about God and those we love to change our wicked ways. For if we are indifferent to the collateral damage our sinful actions cause, then we are playing with fire and likely bound to burn ourselves severely.

Receiving the Word of God is an honor and privilege, but it also comes with great personal responsibility to apply what the Lord teaches. Scripture warns, **"For if we go on sinning deliberately after receiving the knowledge of the truth, there no longer remains a sacrifice for sins, but a fearful expectation of judgment, and a fury of fire that will consume the adversaries" (Hebrews 10:26–27)**. In other words, we cannot choose to sin and act as if God will turn a blind eye. We know what behavior the Lord expects, so we are without excuse on judgment day if we ignore His warnings. **"So whoever knows the right thing to do and fails to do it, for him it is sin" (James 4:17)**. In the end, we cannot be lukewarm with holy Scripture. Rather, we must listen and obey the Spirit's voice to avoid committing sins of indifference.

Application

1. What does it mean to be indifferent or lukewarm towards sin and temptation?

2. How has indifference towards spiritual disciplines plagued your faith journey?

3. Which false idols distract you from quality time with God and tempt you to be apathetic toward personal sin?

4. Which absolute truths of Scripture do you struggle applying most? How so?

5. How has indifference to the needs of others hindered your ability to love and serve like Jesus would?

6. When are you most vulnerable to indifference and portraying an "I don't care!" attitude?

Prayer

Lord, Your Word has changed my life, yet I often get distracted from reading it daily. My prayers are more laundry list requests for personal comfort than intimate conversations with You. I have become calloused to the needs of others and have punted my responsibility to serve rather than obey the Spirit's prompting. Please forgive my indifference and lack of concern for those around me. I do not want to be a man who is self-absorbed and selfish. Rather, help me obey Your Holy Spirit without reservation as I embrace the role of a spiritual leader. Give me wisdom and discernment to lead my family by modeling what determination and intentionality looks like in my spiritual disciplines, so that I can be a Godly example. Amen.

Day 40 - Leadership

> *"Shepherd the flock of God that is among you, exercising oversight, not under compulsion, but willingly, as God would have you; not for shameful gain, but eagerly; not domineering over those in your charge, but being examples to the flock."*
>
> — 1 Peter 5:2–3 —

There is arguably no greater joy, honor, and privilege than being chosen by God to spiritually lead the flock He has given us to shepherd. If we look around, the Lord has placed us in different groups and communities, from our immediate family to Bible study groups at church. We often find ourselves in teams at work, on the field, or in committees where we can make a real difference. Wherever the Lord leads, we have opportunities to step up to the plate and be Godly influences as spiritual leaders. Therefore, we must be sensitive to the Holy Spirit's prompting as we humbly and selflessly shepherd those around us.

The challenge most of us face is overcoming our fears and proactively taking the lead. However, if we publicly proclaim ourselves as Christians, we should be held to a higher standard of righteousness than the world. God expects us to surrender to His authority, obey His Word, and submit to His sovereign will, which means our lives no longer belong to us. Rather, they belong to Christ and are meant to reflect His grace and mercy to those around us. Therefore, when our hearts are aligned with what God cares about and we stand on the absolute truth of Scripture, we will find ourselves isolated and leading a march towards holiness which few men are willing to embrace.

The truth of the matter is we should all be held to a higher standard. There is no reason for us to run and hide from Godly accountability because humility is best learned when others call out our flaws and failures. The key is wearing our faith identity in Christ on our sleeves so that everyone around us is aware of who we are and to whom we belong. However, most men would rather compartmentalize their faith from all other areas of life so they can avoid feeling as if they are constantly being examined under a microscope. However, that is not leadership but cowardice, and we are wise to avoid believing that spiritual leadership is always someone else's job and never ours.

During the 2020 covid pandemic, major corporations were expected to implement strict CDC guidelines for vaccinations in the U.S. It all came to a head when federal mandates were forcing major companies to require vaccinations or face fines. Unfortunately, my employer fell into that group, so I began applying for religious exemption because I did not feel comfortable being injected with the required vaccine or booster shots. Inevitably, the U.S. Supreme Court stepped in at the last minute and put an end to the mandate which eliminated my need for personal exemption. Therefore, I was no longer required to be vaccinated to keep my job.

However, something did not sit right with me. How could I prepare to legally defend myself and then suddenly not be required? It did not seem fair. Therefore, I decided to continue writing my appeal from Scripture's perspective regarding why religious exemption was warranted in this particular case. I not only posted it to my website as a resource for others who were still subject to the vaccine mandate to read and discern, but I also sent it to my human resources department. Certainly, I did not have to, but I felt empowered to finish what I had started and embrace the opportunity God provided to have a deeper faith discussion in corporate America. To me, it was important to lead a respectful dialogue which centered around faith-based decisions in the workplace and the role we have as Christians to stand boldly for what we doctrinally believe.

In many cases, leadership is never easy. In fact, it is quite a lonely endeavor. Persecution and scrutiny come to those who choose to lead, especially when it comes to spiritual headship and practicing what we preach. However, if being a leader were easy, everyone would do it. The truth is we all can and should be leaders in the communities where God has placed us. We just need to reject the enemy's lies which magnify our faults and tempt us to give up. However, it begs the question, what if all Christians took on that attitude? How would our world look if we stopped caring about moral integrity and promoting the need for personal character?

When we humble ourselves and be servant-leaders, marriages are strengthened and children are raised in homes with discipline and boundaries to protect them. The church and home are transformed into mirror images of one another the more we model Jesus' leadership characteristics. Therefore, our duty moving forward is simple. Model the example of Christ in everything we say and do, because the Lord will honor our sacrifice with countless blessings. For when we fulfill the leadership role God gave us long ago in the Garden of Eden, we are empowered to manage our business in the wisdom and discipline of the Lord to the glory of Jesus' name. All we must do is overcome our fears, love those in our sphere of influence, and humbly embrace our leadership role.

Application

1. What are the defining characteristics of an effective leader?
2. In what areas of your life do you consider yourself a leader? How has that role shaped who you are today?
3. Why is it critical to model expected behavior in leadership?
4. What lessons have you learned from those who have abused their leadership privileges?
5. How can you become a better spiritual leader at home?
6. What do you believe those within your sphere of influence would say about your ability to shepherd them spiritually?
7. Why is it critical for a spiritual leader to own his mistakes and confess his sins publicly?

Prayer

Lord, as I reflect upon these past 40-days, I confess that I have a tremendous amount to learn when it comes to personifying the attributes of a Godly man. However, I know that to be an effective leader in my home, community, or in the workplace, I must die to my love of self and humbly surrender control to You. I cannot be the man You call me to be without washing my mind daily with the absolute truth of Your Word. Please help me remove the log from my eye so I can remove the speck from the eyes of those You have gifted me to shepherd. Give me grace when I fail You and courage to change into a Godly leader. Help me admit my mistakes and own my failures with humility. Mold me into the man You call me to be, who loves You and his neighbor as well. Amen.

POSTFACE

The Battle Begins

Thank you for embarking on this devotional journey as we learned how to embrace vulnerability and humble ourselves as Godly men. Keep in mind, these topics are not just a list of character attributes to avoid and learn, but a starting point for us to dive deep into Scripture on our own to glean wisdom and discernment. God's Word can teach us so much about the character of a Godly man if we are willing to listen and obey. Therefore, we are wise to study the Scriptures daily, in prayer and thanksgiving, as we refine our personal character into the image of Christ.

Unfortunately, spiritual warfare will continue to increase despite our best efforts. Satan would love nothing more than for us to forget all we have learned and abandon our post as providers and protectors of our homes. He wants us to backslide into old, sinful patterns and lower our guard, so that he has ample opportunity to exploit the cracks in our armor which we assume are repaired. That is why we must be aware of our weaknesses, and our presumed strengths, because our enemy is eager to weaponize our prideful confidence against us.

Therefore, we cannot allow this devotional journey to come to a climactic end. Rather, we must continually reflect upon these topics to ensure we are not self-deceived to think more highly of ourselves than we ought. Spiritual warfare is not for the faint of heart. Satan knows that if he can tempt us to doubt God's Word, we will easily fall victim to his schemes and isolate ourselves from Biblical truth and accountability. Therefore, we must remain connected to our brothers and sisters in Christ and bathe our minds in the absolute truth of God's Word daily.

One thing we must remember to avoid being discouraged is that spiritual warfare is not something we should run from but embrace. Reason being, Satan does not waste his time, energy, and resources on unbelievers he already controls. He invests his tactics against the saints of God who have chosen to plant a flag in the foundation of God's Word. Sometimes, we think spiritual warfare is sign that the Spirit of God is absent from our lives. On the contrary, spiritual warfare is a sign that we are exactly where God wants to be, because the enemy is scared of the changes we are making to become more Godly men.

Therefore, we must not run and hide from the battle, but embrace the process of sanctification which includes enduring spiritual warfare. Keep in mind, we have nothing to fear but fear itself. Jesus already defeated sin and death on the cross of Calvary when he rose from the grave. However, that does not mean the enemy will not seek to destroy us if given ample opportunity. Therefore, we must constantly be on guard and use the lessons we have learned in **"Attributes of a Godly Man"** to shore up our spiritual defense.

For if we do not surrender to God's authority, obey His Word, and submit to His sovereign will, we will be devoured. Satan is poised and ready to unravel all we have learned these past 40-days because he knows God is doing a mighty work within our hearts to the glory of Jesus' name. Therefore, the time is now to prepare for battle and put on the full armor of God, because spiritual warfare is already upon us! The only question is whether we will turn and fight or surrender in defeat.

https://www.journeyintothewilderness.com

Discipleship Resources

Wilderness Survival, Vol-1 & Vol-2

Men's Bible Study / Discipleship Curriculum

Embark on a journey of survival training deep in the spiritual wilderness of isolation where few men dare to venture. Explore forty personal issues every man deals with in his life and marriage. Embrace the ultimate accountability challenge to become the man, husband, and father God calls you to be by transforming your life and changing your behavior.

"Wilderness Survival" is all about building Godly spiritual disciplines and surrendering to God's authority by examining your heart and filtering it through the absolute truth of His Word. The more you learn to guard your mind, the greater chance you will have of surviving the wilderness seasons of life and marriage, restoring the joy of your salvation, and defeating the enemy once and for all.

About The Author

Daniel Ploof is the author of **"Wilderness Survival, Volume-1 & Volume-2,"** a Bible study and discipleship series designed to help men overcome isolation and become more Godly husbands and fathers. He is also the founder of **Wilderness Survival Training**, a Biblically-based resource platform designed to equip Christian men with wisdom and discernment to guard against spiritual warfare. For more information and free access to resources and devotions, please visit: **https://www.journeyintothewilderness.com**.

Daniel has been married to the love of his life and best friend, Amber, for over twenty-one years. They live outside Nashville, TN, and are the proud parents of four daughters who are their greatest treasures this side of heaven.

www.ingramcontent.com/pod-product-compliance
Lightning Source LLC
Chambersburg PA
CBHW071346080526
44587CB00017B/2985